The Marxist Theory of

nadir –
oppoobrium

pg 45 – Lukacs
perfunctory
58-59 brief description of
epic theatre

MARXIST THEORY AND CONTEMPORARY CAPITALISM

General Editor: John Mepham

This is a new series of texts, of new British books and translations committed to:

the development of Marxist theory

the analysis of contemporary capitalism, its tendencies and contradictions

the record of the struggles to which they give rise

Also in this series:

Charles Bettelheim
The Transition to Socialist Economy

Michel Bosquet
Capitalism in Crisis and Everyday Life

Claudie Broyelle
Women's Liberation In China

Gérard Chaliand
Revolution in the Third World: Myths and Prospects

Carmen Claudin-Urondo
Lenin and the Cultural Revolution

Colin Henfrey and Bernardo Sorj (Eds.)
Chilean Voices: Activists describe their Experiences of the Popular Unity Period

David-Hillel Ruben
Marxism and Materialism: A Study in Marxist Theory of Knowledge

André Gorz (Ed.)
The Division of Labour: The Labour Process and Class Struggle in Modern Capitalism

Tom Clarke and Laurie Clements
Trade Unions under Capitalism

Lucien Sève
Man in Marxist Theory: and the psychology of personality

The Marxist Theory of Art

DAVE LAING

THE HARVESTER PRESS · SUSSEX

HUMANITIES PRESS · NEW JERSEY

First published in Great Britain in 1978 by
THE HARVESTER PRESS LIMITED
Publisher: John Spiers
2 Stanford Terrace, Hassocks, Sussex

and in the USA by
HUMANITIES PRESS INC.
Atlantic Highlands, New Jersey 07716

© Dave Laing, 1978

British Library Cataloguing in Publication Data
Laing, Dave
The Marxist theory of art. — (Marxist theory and contemporary capitalism).
1. Arts 2. Communism and art
I. Title II. Series
700   HX521

ISBN 0-85527-445-X (Cloth)
     0-85527-632-0 (Paper)

Humanities Press Inc.
Library of Congress Cataloging in Publication Data
Laing, Dave.
The Marxist theory of art.
(Marxist theory and contemporary capitalism)
Bibliography: p.
Includes index.
1. Socialism and the arts. I. Title. II. Series.
HX521.L32 1978   335.43'8'7   77-28618
ISBN 0-391-00833-1

Typeset by The Humble Wordsmith, Tonbridge, Kent
Printed in England by
Redwood Burn, Trowbridge & Esher

Contents

Introduction

THE last two decades have seen a greater intensity of activity in the Marxist theory and practice of the arts than at any time since the 1920s in the Soviet Union. That activity has, in turn, been part of a wider emphasis among Marxists, particularly in the capitalist West, on the problems associated with what classical Marxist theory designated the 'ideological superstructure' of the social formation. In particular, the widespread dissemination of the ideas of Antonio Gramsci concerned with questions of revolutionary strategy in countries where ruling-class power is maintained primarily through the electoral consent of the working class, has enabled a new valuation to be made of institutions and practices previously regarded as peripheral to revolutionary struggle.

As a result, Marxist aesthetics today appears, at first sight, to be a luxuriant confusion of ideas and theories. There are Marxist positions which regard classic realism as the only basis for revolutionary art, condemning all modernism and *avant-garde* works as complicit with reaction, and there are others which propose the precise opposite. Some regard the arts as second only to the sciences in the validity of their insights into reality, while for others they are the site of constant ideological struggles.

This situation is rooted in the fundamental absence of a theory of art in Marx's own work. Marx and Engels situated art among those activities of the 'superstructure' which maintained a 'relative autonomy' from the economic base of society, yet were 'in the last instance' determined by it. Isolated hints and occasional comments dealt with aspects of literature as such, some of which (notably Engels' comments on realism) later formed the basis of particular Marxist theories.

The most prominent of these was Soviet socialist realism, which was the only acceptable form of aesthetic theory within the international communist movement for over twenty years, until 1956. The theory itself was the outcome of a long period of debate and struggle in the Soviet Union, following the 1917 Revolution, when the Bolsheviks, like all other Marxists, did not possess an aesthetics which could guide artistic practice in a socialist society.

In fact, it was not until the 1930s that Lukacs and Brecht produced opposing theories capable of guiding a socialist practice of the arts within capitalist society. Until that point, Marxist aesthetics outside the Soviet Union had been undertaken predominantly in order to round off historical materialism as a theory capable of comprehending all social phenomena, even those 'furthest' from the economic base of the social formation.

It is important to understand the fitful and uneven historical development of Marxist aesthetics, as a starting-point for considering its various aspects at the present time. Otherwise, there is the danger of adopting a 'history of ideas' approach, in which disembodied thinkers are seen to consider a logically-determined series of problems, whose solutions comprise a satisfying totality. In fact, the history of Marxist aesthetics is that of a series of responses to pressing problems, which, however far removed from the specific practice of art they appear to be, necessarily imply a preference for one method of artistic production over another.

This book is constructed, in that light, as a map of the field of Marxist aesthetics. In most respects, it does not break new ground, but brings together ideas and material which, for certain reasons, have not been united in a single perspective in English before. The most important of those reasons are the deep political and theoretical divisions which exist between different Marxist approaches to the subject. Often these divisions reflect more general confrontations within Marxism: between 'early Marxists' and 'late Marxists', 'neo-Hegelians' and 'materialists', followers of the 'Moscow line' and the 'Chinese line'. As a result, much of the easily accessible material in English on Marxist aesthetics has presented less than a comprehensive picture of the field and the major unresolved issues within it. One recent anthology ignores Walter Benjamin and Sartre (Craig, 1975), while another sets aside Russian Formalism and French 'structuralism' and semiotics (Solomon, 1973). Neither finds room for Lucien Goldmann. And, for a decade after its publication in 1963, Ernst Fischer's idiosyncratic *The Necessity of Art* was the only general introduction to the field available in English.

The present work is also a general introduction, intended as a structured presentation of the major ideas of the most important trends of thought in the Marxist theory of art. It necessarily neglects many authors on the subject whose views have not seemed either to open up the field in new ways, or to have exerted such influence as to open or close it for others. It also neglects many important artists committed to socialism or Marxism, whose theoretical reflections on their work did not achieve the precision or clarity of Brecht's or Mayakovsky's writings. It is broadly chronological, since the history of the Marxist theory of art has been frequently marked by the sharpening of ideas in conflict and controversy, and it is at those moments that the political implications of opposing views are most clearly to be seen. The exceptions to that structure are the final two chapters which deal with a particular area of study (the so-called popular arts and mass-media) and the various views on Marxist aesthetics to be found within Anglo-American Marxist traditions. This is because the book is intended not only as an introduction to a field of academic or contemplative study, but also to be of use to those in the English-speaking world who find themselves actively involved in the field of culture and the arts, amongst which, it seems to me, those 'mass media' are now of primary strategic importance and also the least explored by an intellectual tradition whose inherent bias has generally been towards literature as the paradigm of the arts.

In introducing the ideas of the various authors, I have attempted to maintain a position of neutrality, and then to present what seem to be the most cogent criticisms of those ideas from other Marxist perspectives. It may nevertheless be of value to the reader to be aware of the author's own attitude towards his subject. This is that the most productive aspects of Marxist aesthetics are those which question its dependence on inherited nineteenth-century concepts of 'art' and of 'realism', and those which orientate it towards a practice of art which can locate itself in relation to continuing political and ideological struggles taking place elsewhere in society.

From this perspective, certain key questions seem to recur amongst the various phases of the history described in this book. They include: the place and 'special character' of art as a social practice in relationship to the economic base; its definition as a mode of 'expression' or one of 'production'; and the possibility or impossibility of a fruitful conjunction of Marxism and Freudianism in a theory of art which retains a concept of political contradiction at its centre.

Chapter One

ORIGINS OF AN AESTHETIC

IN a 1967 account of his own intellectual development, Georg Lukacs wrote that it was not until the 1930s that 'an independent and integral Marxist aesthetic' was expounded. Earlier communist writers had not 'thought of aesthetics as a vital part of the Marxist system'. They had drawn instead on other, non-Marxist ideas as the source of their view of art.[1]

For Lukacs, the decisive factor which made a Marxist aesthetic now possible was the publication of certain of Marx's early writings for the first time, notably the *Economic and Philosophical Manuscripts* of 1844.

> 'While most of the leaders of the Second International saw him exclusively, or at least primarily, as the man who revolutionised economics, we now started to understand that a new era had begun with him in the whole history of human thought.'[2]

During the early 1930s, Lukacs worked in Moscow at the Marx-Engels Institute. It was one of his fellow-workers there, Mikhail Lifshitz, who first edited a selection of material by Marx and Engels on art and literature, as well as producing the first study of Marx's aesthetics, *The Philosophy of Art of Karl Marx* (1973). It concentrated principally on those newly published works of the 1840s which were particularly rich in the discussion of aesthetic issues. In these early writings, Marx was considering and criticising the philosophical influences of the German tradition, in whose work aesthetic questions were frequently of central significance.

Many subsequent reconstructions of an aesthetic from within the works of Marx and Engels have followed

1

Lifshitz in focusing on formulations within these early works and arguing for a continuity between them and the less frequent and more fragmentary references to artistic issues as the focus of Marx's attention shifted from philosophy to political economy in the later writings. Stefan Morawski (in Marx & Engels, 1974) has usefully divided the scattered comments on aesthetics into 'themes', 'observations' and 'remarks', where the second and third categories denote half-finished or hardly begun discussions of artistic issues.[3] In both the earlier and later works, art is frequently accorded a special status amongst social activity in general. In the philosophical writings of the 1840s, it tends to assume a privileged role in discussions of 'Man' in general as a 'species-being', where the aesthetic sense, or the creativity of the artist prefigures or acts as a guide to the nature of an unalienated existence. As Marx turns from philosophy to theory, this sense of the special character of art is subsumed into key test cases for the explanatory range of Marxist theory, notably in the area of the relations between the economic base and the superstructure of the social formation.

For Marxist authors who consider the earlier works to be discontinuous with the mature theory, it is here that the starting point for an exposition of artistic issues is to be found. Art is then seen as a particular sector of the ideological level of the superstructure, whose relations of dependence and independence are to be discovered. A third chronological phase of aesthetic comment, belonging entirely to Engels, has also been influential among later Marxists. This comprised his prescriptive remarks on the character of 'realist' art in letters written during the 1880s. These remarks would later come to occupy a central place in the doctrine of socialist realism in the Soviet Union.

The anthologies of Marx and Engels *On Literature And Art* available in English have tended to group the material according to categories of aesthetic thought determined by the anthologists and their own view of Marxism.

They range from the orthodox socialist realist position, which organises the material along historical lines, from 'Origins of Art' to 'Literary History', (*Marx & Engels*, Bombay, 1956), to selections aimed at locating a utopian dimension in art (Solomon, 1973). The first type stresses the implication of art in the epoch of its production, while the second emphasises the qualities of art which enable it to point beyond that epoch.

Both, nevertheless, share the view that there is an integral aesthetic to be found in Marx and Engels, and that it can, finally, be read off from what the anthologist in question considers to be the principal features of the general theoretical work of the founders of Marxism. The subsequent history of Marxist aesthetics (not to mention marxist thought in general) suggests, however, that the importance of these aesthetic texts may lie more in their signalling of problematic areas to be worked on further, rather than the exposition of a consistent system. Furthermore, since few of these texts are themselves discrete essays or letters, but interpolations into texts primarily concerned with other issues, the context of the utterance becomes of major importance in determining its significance. In order to survey the texts of Marx and Engels, I have therefore adopted a chronological approach.

1. MARX AND ENGELS ON ART

As students and until 1844, Karl Marx (1818-1883) and Friedrich Engels (1820-1895) worked strictly within the domain of German classical philosophy, where art and philosophy were intimately bound up with the movement of history as a whole. Both the romanticism of Schiller and Fichte and the Hegelian system contrasted the organic unity of classical Greece with the atomised, egotistical character of contemporary bourgeois society, which was inimical to great art. In 1842, Marx wrote: "If we consider the gods and heroes of Greek art without religious or aesthetic prejudices, we find in them nothing which could not exist in the pulsations of nature. Indeed, these images are artistic only as they portray beautiful human mores in a splendid integrated form.'[4]

This observation recurs in a famous crux of Marx's writing fifteen years later, when he had shifted decisively away from his early philosophical positions. By 1842, however, Marx had already moved beyond the Romanticism which influenced his youthful attempts at poetry to a Left Hegelian standpoint, which accepted the outlines of Hegel's system but rejected its author's political conservatism. Marx's dissertation on the Greek philosopher Epicurus maintained the contrast between the art of Greece and Rome (which is characterised in much the same terms as contemporary Germany), but regarded the Epicurean notion of atomism in a positive light. For Hegel, this idea marked the collapse of the social cohesion of Greece, while Marx found in it an enlightened self-interest which was the real basis of communality.

At this period, too, Marx encountered the idea of fetishism in a critique of Christian art by the art historian Grund. In contrast to the reflection of nature and 'beautiful human mores' in Greek sculpture, 'the fetishistic character of religion is demonstrated by the fact that it worships the material aspect of things, endowing them with the qualities of man himself.'[5] This aesthetic concept of fetishism is clearly one source of the later concept of alienation, which would, in 1844, be central to Marx's political philosophy.

In 1842, Marx became editor of the *Rheinische Zeitung*, in which he wrote a series of articles on censorship, the freedom of the press and the writer's craft. With considerable polemical skill, he ridiculed the censor's distinction between 'competent' and 'incompetent' writing, and argued that 'the first freedom of the press consists in its not being a business.' The writer, furthermore, is distinguished by the fact that in no sense does he 'regard his works as a *means*. They are *ends in themselves*; so little are they means for him and others that, when necessary, he sacrifices *his* existence to *theirs* . . .'.[6] By 'writing as a means' Marx is here referring to writing as simply a way of making a living, with the implicit corollory that such writers become hired hacks, willing to accept censorship. His statement can then be read as an endorsement of committed writing in the most general sense, and also as claiming a 'free' independent status for the genuine writer, a notion his later work would implicitly repudiate.

1844 found Marx working on the *Economic and Philosophical Manuscripts*, the first great watershed in his development, where he used the humanist materialism of Feuerbach to emancipate his thought from Hegelian idealism. In these fragmentary texts, Marx argues persistently that the elements of human society and of man's consciousness are the product of human activity itself and not some external force. And, since the concept of beauty and artistic practice itself are among those elements which distinguish man as a species, it is crucial to establish their origins in human activity itself. The following is a key passage:

> Only through the objectively unfolded richness of man's essential being is the richness of subjective *human* sensibility (a musical ear, an eye for beauty of form — in short, *senses* capable of human gratifications, senses confirming themselves as essential power of *man*) either cultivated or brought into being . . . The forming of the five senses is a labour of the entire history of the world down to the present.[7]

But this humanist paean is counterpointed by the awareness that 'the *sense* caught up in crude practical need has only a restricted sense'. In a class society under the domination of money (it is here that Marx quotes copiously from Shakespeare and Goethe on the power of money to estrange men from themselves), the full development of the five senses is impossible: 'The care-burdened man in need has no sense for the finest play.'

In the same year, 1844, Engels was writing a contrasting

piece of aesthetics. In an article for the English Chartist newspaper, *New Moral World*, on "Rapid Progress Of Communism In Germany', he described in detail the painting *The Silesian Weavers* by Hubner, 'which has made a more effectual Socialist agitation than a hundred pamphlets might have done'.[8] *The Holy Family* (1845) was the major collaboration of Marx and Engels, and included an extended piece of literary criticism which combined the specificity of Engels' 1844 article with a more general philosophical critique. The object of the text was to analyse an essay by the Young Hegelian Szeliga praising Eugène Sue's novel *Mysteries Of Paris* for its portrayal of lower-class life. Marx and Engels set out to show how both author and critic share an ideology of bourgeois romanticism which dominates and determines the supposed realism of the melodramatic novel. They show how Rudolph, the book's hero, remains entirely within the moral world of the bourgeoisie: 'Rudolph captures this criminal. He wants to reform him critically and set him as an example for the *world of law*. He quarrels with the world of law not over '*punishment*' itself, but over *kinds* and *methods* of punishment . . .'.[9] There is a similar fatal limitation in the portrayal of the character of Rigoletto:

> In her Eugène Sue portrayed that admirable human character, the Parisian grisette. However, out of his devotion to the bourgeoisie and his own transcendentalism, he was forced to idealise her from a moral standpoint. He had to extenuate the salient trait of Rigoletto's character and situation: her disdain of marriage, her naïve relations with the student and the worker. Yet it is precisely these naïve relations which place her in truly human contrast with the hypocritical, avaricious, egotistical bourgeois wife, and the entire bourgeois world, that is to say, the entire official world.[10]

The Holy Family, of course, is a polemical political pamphlet, not principally a work of aesthetics. Nevertheless, these passages indicate how it contains, in practical form, a concept of the relationship between art and authorial ideology which Engels would return to in later years and which would preoccupy later writers on the subject. In particular the Rigoletto passage indicates the existence of a contradiction between the text (the actions and relationships of the character) and the author's conscious attempts to 'explain' it.

The German Ideology (1846) marks a decisive shift from the critique of philosophy to a preliminary statement of Marx and Engels' theory of historical materialism in which 'life is not determined by consciousness, but consciousness by life' and 'the ideas of the ruling class are in every epoch the ruling ideas'. It also brings to the fore the concept of the division of labour in class societies, whose origin is in the split between physical and mental work. One of the aims of communism is the abolition of this division of labour and of specialisation, in the artistic field as well as elsewhere. "In a communist society there are no painters but at most people who engage in painting among other activities."[11]

Two 1847 texts by Engels on individual writers indicate the changing nature of his and Marx's thought at this period. A section of his *German Socialism in Verse and Prose* analyses Goethe's 'double relation to the German society of his time'. It is a restless passage, defining this contradiction at the heart of Goethe's work in different ways, but fundamentally as a split between his artistic genius and his conservative life in making peace with the *status quo* in the Germany of his time. But in an article on a lesser writer, the French politician Lamartine, Engels employs the terminology of class analysis to locate precisely the source of the subject's ideology:

> M. de Lamartine proves himself, both under a social and political point of view, the faithful representative of the small tradesman, the inferior bourgeoisie, and who shares in the illusion particular to this class: that he represents the working people.[12]

In a famous formulation from *The Eighteenth Brumaire Of Louis Bonaparte* (1852), Marx fully developed this relation between ideology and class, thereby inaugurating a whole strand of Marxist cultural analysis. He argued that the French Social Democrats of the time held a petty bourgeois ideology, even though they were not necessarily shopkeepers or 'enthusiastic champions of shopkeepers'. Instead:

> what makes them representatives of the petty bourgeoisie is the fact that in their minds they do not get beyond the limits which the latter do not get beyond in life, that they are constantly driven, theoretically, to the same problems and solutions to which material interest and social position drive the latter practically. This is, in general, the relationship between the political and literary representatives of a class and the class they represent.[13]

The importance of this remark is that it offers, for the first time, an account of the structure of the connection between ideology and social class, superstructure and base. The connection suggested is one of an *homology* between the two, rather than a simple reflection or expression of base by superstructure.

A year earlier, in an article for the *New York Times*, Engels had introduced into the Marxist *oeuvre* another term which would reverberate through later Marxist debates: the notion of 'tendency' writing. He uses it here to describe an inferior trend in German literature during the 1840s: 'It became more and more the habit, particularly of the inferior sort of literati, to make up for the want of cleverness in their productions by political allusions which were sure to attract attention.'[14] 'Tendency' is here implicitly opposed to genuine or great art, the nature of which is elucidated in an exchange of letters between Marx and Engels and the German communist, Ferdinand Lassalle, in 1859. Lassalle had written a tragic drama, *Franz von Sickingen*, dealing with a major uprising during the Reformation in Germany. The insurgent peasants were led by the petty nobility, personified in the tragic hero, von Sickingen.

Frederick Jameson (1971) has pointed out the influential nature of Marx and Engels' critique for future Marxist criticism in general, and for Georg Lukacs in particular, a fact which Lukacs acknowledges in his 1967 autobiographical essay. Marx and Engels argue that the source of the tragedy in history lay not in a character flaw in von Sickingen, as Lassalle proposes, but in the objective nature of the class forces involved in the rebellion. The petty nobility's alliance with the peasants failed because of a clash of class interests. 'As the play stands,' writes Jameson,

> the character of Sickingen does not typify the real historical dilemma, the situation of the play does not give a genuine model of the forces at work during the period; and Marx and Engels show how all the formal weaknesses of the play (its endless speechifying, its reminiscences of Schiller rather than Shakespeare) flow from the more fundamental weakness, the inadequacy of the work to its raw material.[15]

Implicit here is a critique similar to that made of Eugène Sue. There too, the author's ideological and artistic grasp (the two are not actually distinguished) was defective in its ability to perceive the totality of forces at work in the situation. Sue could not grasp that aspect of the Parisian *lumpenproletariat* that negated bourgeois society, and Lassalle mistakes an objective 'tragedy' for an individual one.

Central to this critique is a key term which links the aesthetic work with its 'raw material' — typicality. Here, Engels congratulates Lassalle on his characterisation:

> the principal characters are representatives of distinct classes and tendencies and hence definite ideas of their time, and the motives of their actions are to be found not in trivial individual desires but in the historical stream on which they are carried.[16]

This critique of Lassalle provides the basic concepts Engels would go on to deploy in his later letters on realism, but the period up to Marx's death in 1883 was marked by a number of methodological issues in the elaboration of the base/superstructure relationship at a theoretical level, one of which has remained an enigma for Marxist aesthetics ever since.

The problem to be resolved occurs in the *Introduction to the Critique of Political Economy* (1857). Marx is discussing the relationship between art and the society which produced it. Greek art, he points out, could not be produced in the age of steam engines and printing presses, since its basis was a system of mythology which functioned to dominate nature through the imagination, since it was not possible to do so in reality:

> But the difficulty does not lie in understanding that the Greek art and epos are bound up with certain forms of development. It rather lies in understanding why they still afford us aesthetic enjoyment and in certain respects prevail as the standard and model beyond attainment.[17]

Max Raphael (1968) suggested that Marx had here 'come to a problem he could not solve', since the solution proposed by Marx himself seemed to contradict his historical materialist position. Echoing the idealist admiration for the Greeks of his own philosophical past, he wrote: 'Why should the historical childhood of humanity, where it had obtained its most beautiful development, not exert an eternal charm as an age that will never return?'

But if the language is that of idealism, could the answer nevertheless contain a Marxist element, or is this simply a sudden regression on Marx's part? Broadly speaking, there are two kinds of positive answer which later Marxists have put: that Greek society possessed certain features inherently superior to the European class societies which succeeded it, and therefore its art retained certain essential human values missing from feudalism and capitalism where the commodity-form is dominant (e.g. Lifshitz), or that great art of any period inherently retains the ability to outlive its origins. The latter argument can take two forms, either insisting on the realism of a work's portrayal of the historical moment of its production (thus Marx and Engels on Lassalle), or on its possession of a harmonious perfection of form. This final argument can also be linked with Lifshitz's view, that Greek society was inherently superior to later class societies.

To adopt these positions, is however, to grant art a special status within the ideological superstructure, as superior to law, philosophy or religion, whose existence is seen within Marxism as either entirely dependent on the rule of one specific class, or as adopted by successive ruling classes in order to cloak themselves with legitimate authority. This perspective on the problem suggests an alternative solution, proposed by Hans Hess (1973). Hess argues that while Marx acknowledges that the production of art is historically 'bound up with certain forms of social development', so too is its consumption or reception. Thus Marx failed to see that the modern admiration for Greek art owed less to some trans-historical essence in the works themselves than to the aesthetic ideologies or philosophies prevailing in modern societies and their corresponding cultural institutions. Within these, according to Hess, 'the spectator or believer is meant to be overawed, the work of art is a piece of establishment furniture, which makes it clear where power resides'.

In fact, four years after he wrote his comments on Greek art, Marx himself acknowledged the survival of artistic forms in a context where their use or meaning had changed. Lassalle had written to him about the adoption, in a mistaken way, of classical dramatic forms by modern authors. In reply Marx wrote that the existence of such a phenomenon, in the face of contemporary scholarship, which pointed out the misunderstandings on the part of modern dramatists, was due to its answering the artistic need of the time. It was no less an authentic bourgeois drama because its practitioners adopted forms from past societies.

In addition to the texts on art as an aspect of the super-structure (a term introduced by Marx in his 1859 *Preface To a Contribution To a Critique of Political Economy*), the major works of political economy, *Capital* and *Theories Of Surplus Value*, contain various references to artistic production as a branch of production in general, predominantly in relation to the distinction between productive and un-productive labour within capitalism. The precise ground of that distinction remains a subject of debate among Marxist economists and it is symptomatic that in places Marx's use of the artistic example involves a return to the 1842 designation of the true writer as one who somehow remains unimplicated in the necessities of the capitalist relations of production. Thus: "A writer is a productive labourer not in so far as he produces ideas, but in so far as he enriches the publisher who publishes his works, or if he is a wage-labourer for a capitalist.'[18] Elsewhere, this basic definition of productive labour as that which generates surplus-value is extended to suggest that there are therefore two kinds of writer. Milton 'produced *Paradise Lost* for the same reason that a silk-worm produces silk. It was an activity of his nature'. In contrast, there is 'the literary proletarian of Leipzig who fabricates books under the direction of his publisher' and whose product is 'from the outset subsumed under capital'.[19] As with the issue of the survival of Greek art, Marx has here signalled a problem rather than solved it. This comment, apart from attempting to find an equivalent at the level of political economy for a distinction at the level of aesthetics, opens up the whole area of an artist's work and of the significance of its means of (mass) production and distribution as a commodity. Like many others, however, it was not a theme Marx was able to pursue. Like so much else he had intended, his book on art remained unwritten.

2. CLARIFYING THE AESTHETIC: ENGELS AND PLEKHANOV

Even before Marx's death, his ideas had begun to gain support within the European socialist movement, notably in Germany. In the decade afterwards, Marxist-influenced parties moved ahead even more quickly. As the remaining founder of the theory, Engels was faced with the urgent task of explaining the principles and politics underlying *Capital*, in the face of misrepresentation and oversimplification by friend and enemy alike.

One major theme of his writings in these years was the

struggle against 'determinist' interpretations of Marx's ideas, which tended to reduce all superstructural elements to simple epiphenomena of the economic base. His famous series of letters on this question, however, do little more than assert the mutual determination of base and super-structure, with the latter possessing a 'relative autonomy' and the former a power of 'determination in the last instance'.[20] Yet, despite some specific analyses designed to show these factors at work, there remained 'an absence, on the theoretical plane, of any mechanism to connect the determination in the last instance by the economy and the relative autonomy of the superstructures' (G. Stedman Jones, 1973).

One example of the ability of Engels to demonstrate the creativity of his Marxist approach came in a letter to Ernst of 1890. The point at issue is the emergence in Norway of Ibsen's plays dealing with the 'woman question'. Engels takes Ernst to task for designating Ibsen's works as 'petty bourgeois in an abstract manner'. He points out, in a brief comparison of Germany and Norway, that in the latter the intermediate classes play a more progressive role because of the country's particular political and economic history; 'The Norwegian petty bourgeois is the son of a free peasant, and for this reason he is a man compared to the miserable German philistine.'[21] Ibsen as a writer therefore cannot go beyond the horizons by which the petty bour-geoisie are limited in practice, but his work is nevertheless progressive since this class continues to play a progressive social role in Norway.

A final aspect of Engels' activity in this last phase has since assumed a major position in Marxist aesthetics, even though it consists of two letters only: those to Minna Kautsky (1885) and Margaret Harkness (1888), in which he comments on the nature of realism in fiction. The letter to Harkness includes a passage in praise of Balzac in which Engels mentions the ability of a novelist's realist practice to go beyond his conscious sympathies for 'a class doomed to extinction' and to write with 'undisguised admiration' of his 'bitterest political antagonists', 'the real men of the future'.[22] This Engels calls the *triumph of realism*, the ability of art to transcend the limitations of a particular ideology. In contrast, Engels posits 'tendency' writing, in which the artist's conscious declaration of allegiance can destroy the possibility of any artistic effect on the reader. 'Realism', he sums up, 'to my mind, implies, beside truth of detail, the truthful reproduction of typical characters under typical circumstances.' It was a sentence which would be committed to memory by generations of writers and critics in the age of socialist realism.

One important feature of the international growth of Marxism at the end of the nineteenth century was the emergence within the nascent Marxist parties of various countries of leading intellectuals whose role was broadly similar to that of Engels in the last decade of his life. They sought to establish Marxism within their own national culture as a unified system of thought, able to deal with phenomena at all levels of the social structure. Among this first generation of Marxists in Europe, the two most out-standing figures outside Germany — where the special status of Engels and the size of the movement led to a certain 'division of labour' among party intellectuals — were the Italian Antonio Labriola and the Russian Georgi Plekhanov.

Labriola was Professor of Philosophy at Rome University when he became a Marxist in the 1880s. His *Essays On The Materialist Conception Of History* (1895-6) represented the first synthesis of the Marxist world-view after Engels, and paid particular attention to the issues of the superstructure. He distinguished those aspects which were more or less direct 'projections' of economic conditions (law, politics), from the less direct, which included science, art and religion. About the latter he wrote:

> . . . in artistic or religious production the mediation from the conditions to the products is very complicated, and . . . men,

while living in society, do not thereby cease to live alone by themselves in nature, and to receive from it occasion and material for
curiosity and for imagination.[23]

The first part of this statement reiterates the anti-reduc-
tionist warnings of the later Engels, but the second introduces a new theme which Labriola pursues in his discussion of art and religion. Man's relationship with nature and
his biological aspect which links him with nature
represent an important material determinant of social life.
As Timpanero (1974) puts it: 'though they are not actually
eternal, these aspects are nevertheless *long-lasting*; that is to
say, they have, relative to the existence of the human
species, much greater stability than historical or social
institutions.' For Labriola, the relatively important role of
these 'long-lasting' factors is a major reason why art is both
'more distant' from the social base, and also why it can
outlast its moment of origin. He thus provides a different
perspective on Marx's question about the survival of Greek
art.

The discussion of the concept of beauty in Plekhanov's
Art and Social Life includes a similar point, that the idea of
beauty prevailing in society at any particular time is the
product of both 'biological' and historical conditions.
Plekhanov (1856-1918) was a founder of the Russian Social-
Democratic Party and known as the 'Father of Russian
Marxism'. Until the rise of Lenin and the split between
Bolsheviks and Mensheviks, he was acknowledged as the
theoretical leader of Russian communism. He nevertheless
retained an international reputation as an ideologist, notably in the field of aesthetics: *Art And Social Life*, written
in 1912-13, remained a major text in the field for over two
decades, until the publication of Marx's early works and
the scholarship of Lifshitz and Lukacs inaugurated a different tradition.

Like Marx and Engels, Plekhanov was a political refugee
for much of his life, and his knowledge of artistic trends
was similarly encyclopedic. *Art and Social Life* concerns

itself with both French and Russian art in taking up certain questions of the day, notably that of 'art for art's sake'. This trend in art, he concludes, 'arises when artists and people keenly interested in art are hopelessly at odds with their social environment.' Similarly, the alternative position, that of utilitarian art, is always preferred by political authority, since 'it is in its interest to harness all ideologies to the service of the cause which it serves itself. And since political authority, although sometimes revolutionary, is most often conservative and even reactionary, it would be clearly wrong to think that the utilitarian view of art is shared principally by revolutionaries, or by people of advanced mind generally.'[24]

Having made this somewhat unexpected beginning, Plekhanov moves to the attack against 'art for art's sake' for its lack of 'content'. All artistic productions contain ideas, and the merit of a work lies in the loftiness of its content, the extent to which it recognises the major social trends of its time. Thus far, Plekhanov had developed a Marxist sociology of art, relating different artistic ideologies to their social context. There was, however, a gap between this explanatory level, and a level of judgement or prescription of successful artistic work from the Marxist point of view. When challenged by Lunacharsky that he seemed to accept an absolute criterion of beauty, he replied that while such a criterion was of course relative and historically determined, there could still be an

> objective possibility of judging whether a given artistic design has been well executed or not. If what he portrays in his picture really does resemble such a woman, we shall say that he has succeeded in painting a good picture. But if, instead of a woman wearing a blue dress, we see on his canvas several stereometric figures more or less thickly and more or less crudely tinted here and there with blue colour, we shall say that whatever he has painted, it certainly is not a good picture.'[25]

The description is of a cubist painting by Fernand Léger, who, ironically, would later become a committed, socialist artist. The passage itself prefigures the coming storm in

Russia, a decade after it was written, when the relationship of modernist art to a communist ideology was posed in immediate, practical form.

This lack of a genuinely Marxist aesthetics of intervention and criticism to complement a well-developed sociology of art was not unique to Plekhanov amongst the earliest Marxists. In Germany, Franz Mehring, Marx's biographer, wrote copiously for the Party press on literary and artistic matters, but mostly in order to introduce the working class to their 'heritage', classic German literature. He also developed a concept of art as 'a peculiar and aboriginal capacity of mankind', which in the Stalinist 1930s would bring a posthumous denunciation of him for 'literary Trotskyism' from Georg Lukacs.

It can be argued, too, that this lack is apparent in the aesthetic writings of Marx and Engels themselves. Thus Max Raphael wrote that in a period of transition:

> . . . two attitudes are possible. One is to take advantage of the emergent forces of the new order with a view to undermining it, to affirm it in order to drive it beyond itself; this is the active, militant, revolutionary attitude. The other clings to the past, is retrospective or romantic, bewails or acknowledges the decline, asserts that the will to live is gone — in short it is the passive attitude. Where economic, political and social questions were at stake, Marx took the first attitude; in questions of art he took neither.[26]

Exceptions can be found to this stricture, notably the debate on Lassalle's play and Engels' comments on realism. Yet, despite their own immense interest in literature (Prawar, 1977), Marx and Engels never managed to present an integral theory of it, which would indicate a practice of art consonant with revolutionary politics or ideas. There were, of course, more urgent tasks. In the present century, the 'active, militant revolutionary' attitude has been demanded for artistic matters, so that an interventionist strategy could be developed, either after the conquest of power (Russia after 1917) or as part of a continuing struggle (Germany in the 1930s, China in the 1940s). In these situations, the work of Marx and Engels on art pointed to problems, rather than providing solutions. Their writings were necessarily supplemented by new work.

On the other hand, Marxist aesthetics still has a passive, contemplative side. In a 1968 interview, Louis Althusser spoke of the problem in relation to philosophy: 'It is not easy to become a Marxist-Leninist philosopher. Like every 'intellectual', a philosophy teacher is a petty-bourgeois. When he opens his mouth it is petty-bourgeois ideology which speaks. Its resources and ruses are infinite.'[27] This situation is probably at least as serious in the field of literature and art, notably in Western Europe and amongst academics. For, as long as the distance between the arts and political struggle is seen to be immense, it is possible for Marxism to become institutionalised as an alternative version of the conventional discourses on the arts, albeit from the left. Similarly, there can be a temptation to conflate the undoubted specific effectivity of art with the privileged and prestigious status accorded it in the official cultural ideologies of capitalist societies. In this way, via certain aspects of Marx's early writings, art can seem to float above the superstructures, hardly hampered by the exigencies of ideology and class.

The legacy of Marx and Engels on art and literature is thus not unambiguous. Over a period of fifty years, a whole range of opinions, and theoretical hints are deployed in an equally wide range of contexts. Undoubtedly, certain emphases recur, the most important being the special status conferred on the artistic by Marx and Engels. But even here, ambiguity remains. Is that special status a sign that for them art possessed a greater autonomy from the ideological than law, or politics, or simply an indication that the complexity of the relationship between base and superstructure rendered each department of the superstructure a 'special case' as well? This and other lacunae in Marx and Engels were to define the terrain of much later debate among marxists on aesthetic questions.

BIBLIOGRAPHICAL NOTES

There are a number of selections from Marx and Engels on literature and art published either in Moscow or by the publishing houses of various Communist Parties. Of the 'unofficial' selections, *Marx & Engels* (1974) is the best, with its lengthy introduction by Stefan Morawski. Solomon (1974) has a more unusual selection, including a section on utopianism, a continuing theme of his anthology.

Lifshitz (1973), Demetz (1967) and Lukacs (1970) provide detailed commentaries on Marx and Engels' aesthetic thought. For a later Soviet critique of Plekhanov, see Rosenthal (1976).

Chapter Two

SOCIALIST REALISM AND THE SOCIAL COMMAND

MOST recent commentators on Marxist aesthetics outside the socialist countries have passed over the issue of socialist realism with hurried denunciations. Ernst Fischer (1963) felt that although the concept was 'perfectly valid in itself' it had been so abused in practice that it would be better to substitute the term 'socialist art'. Solomon (1974), terming the theory 'Zhdanovism', suggests that it has no roots in Marxism, but has more to do with sexual repression.[1]

Yet socialist realism as the theory of the Marxist practice of art remains influential, and not entirely because it has the weight of the State behind it in nearly every socialist country. It can be legitimately traced back to Marx and Engels and, perhaps more significantly, it reiterates deep-rooted notions of realism which have been powerful influences in European culture for over a century. It did not, however, emerge in an untroubled manner to become the aesthetic counterpart of orthodox Marxism. Its proclamation as such in 1934 was the outcome of a period of ceaseless debate and struggle about the character of socialist art which began immediately after the Russian Revolution of 1917. During the course of those seventeen years, nearly every controversial issue which has exercised later Marxist writers on aesthetics emerged in one form or another.

1. CULTURE AND ART IN LENIN

Labriola and Plekhanov had tried to systematise the hints and generalisations of Marx and Engels into a general theory, but the terms of the Soviet debates in their earliest forms marked a sharp break with that approach. The

20

parallel is with Lenin's break in Marxist thought, his elaboration of a Marxist political practice which was based on
the theory of historical materialism but distinct from it. In
aesthetics, earlier Marxists had been contemplative, not
attempting a *systematic* evaluation of artistic methods in
terms of the struggle for socialism. Instead art was
'decoded' to determine in what way it related to the underlying social reality. Among the few pronouncements on the
political place of art was this, by Kautsky, quoted with dis-
approval by a recent Soviet critic:

> . . . communism in material production, anarchy in intellectual
> production, this is the form of the socialist means of production,
> to which the rule of the proletariat leads by virtue of economic
> laws.[2]

Like Lenin, the Russian artists and critics had to take up
an interventionist, not a contemplative role in 1917. Marx
had said that in every epoch the ruling ideas were those of
the ruling class. Now that the proletariat was the ruling
class, how were its ideas to be reflected in the field of
culture? The essays of Plekhanov and Mehring offered no
guidance, and Kautsky's comment, in a propagandist pamphlet about the nature of the future socialist society,
seemed complacent in a context of Civil War when the
hegemony of the old order was far from defeated.

In the event, the initial positions after 1917 were drawn
from a variety of sources, within and outside the Marxist
movement. Lenin's own statements on cultural issues did
not at this stage play a large role in the debates, principally
because the Party itself did not take a hand until 1920. The
resolution of that year explained:

> If our Party has not up to now interfered in this matter, this may
> be explained only by the fact that it has been engaged in military
> affairs at the front and has not therefore always been able to
> devote the necessary attention to these important questions.[3]

Nevertheless, Lenin's views on the role of artistic work
within the cultural sphere during the immediate post-
revolutionary period had an effect on the work carried out

by Narkompros, the cultural and educational apparatus headed by Lunacharsky. And later, in the construction of the theory of socialist realism, certain of Lenin's pre-revolutionary postulates were cited.

The most important of these was the principle of '*partynost*' (partisanship), which was first stated in his 1905 article 'Party Organisation and Party Literature'.[4] This text has since been the object of controversy, not least on the part of Marxists who have wanted to dissociate themselves (and Lenin) from Soviet socialist realism. Two arguments have been advanced to support such an interpretation: (a) that the context of the piece was specific to Russia in 1905 and its instructions cannot be applied wholesale elsewhere; (b) that the article refers to political and theoretical writing, and not to literary work.

The context is certainly important. The article was written at a moment when the Tsarist government was relaxing its restrictions on the press. Until this point, no paper which was openly tied to a political party was allowed to publish legally. In this way, Lenin writes, 'the question of the party and the non-party press was decided extremely simply and in an extremely false and abnormal way'. The important aspect, for Lenin, was that this situation had made it possible for socialist writers to contribute to the legal press in a totally individualistic and undisciplined manner. They had thus drifted into bad bourgeois habits as writers. Now, with relaxed censorship, it was possible to have a press that was 'nine-tenths' a party press.

Lenin goes on to define the 'principle of party literature' that such a press should adopt:

> It is not simply that, for the socialist proletariat, literature cannot be a means of enriching individuals or groups; it cannot, in fact, be an individual undertaking independent of the common cause of the proletariat. Down with non-partisan writers! Down with literary supermen! Literature must become *part* of the common cause of the proletariat, a 'cog and screw' of one single great Social Democratic mechanism set in motion by the entire politically-conscious vanguard of the entire working class.

Lenin then qualifies this somewhat bald statement by allowing that:

> In this field greater scope must undoubtedly be allowed for personal initiative, individual inclination, thought and fantasy, form and content. All this is undeniable; but all this simply shows that the literary side of the proletarian party cannot be mechanically identified with its other sides.

Clearly, this is an argument to do with political strategy in a bourgeois society. Yet, elsewhere in the article, Lenin makes it plain that he is positing not only the need for a certain kind of political commitment on the part of the writer, but also a decisive change in the *relations of literary production*. The integration of writing into the 'mechanism' of the Party, he says, will 'cut the ground from under the old semi-Oblomov, semi-shopkeeper Russian principle: the writer does the writing, the reader does the reading.' With this arresting phrase, Lenin pinpoints the petty-bourgeois nature of the writer under capitalism: his individualism, which leads to a lack of responsibility for the character of his readership under the guise of the idea of 'free expression', and the hollowness of that freedom when the writer is bound to his 'bourgeois publisher' and 'bourgeois public, which demands that you provide it with pornography in novels and paintings, and prostitution as a "supplement" to "sacred" scenic art.'

Because this argument implies a contrasting situation for the writer to that imposed by capitalist society, the application of Lenin's argument to art in a post-revolutionary society would seem to be legitimate. And his notion of a literature *'openly* linked to the proletariat' looks forward to the concept of 'socialist realism' and to the 'social command' which was central to the ideas of Mayakovsky and his co-thinkers of the 'Lef' group in the 1920s.

What of the statement that Lenin is concerned only with political articles and not 'creative' writing in this essay? The references to 'thought and fantasy, form and content' indicate that, to some degree, novelists and painters are included along with essayists and philosophers. But what is important about Lenin's position is that he makes no clear cut distinction between the various kinds of writing. All are part of a continuum, in which what they have in common is held to be more important than their differences.

Much has been made of Lenin's aesthetic 'philistinism' in the past (the notorious comment on Beethoven, for instance),[5] and it might be tempting to explain this elision of fiction and journalism by reference to that fact. But there are deep and important ideological roots to such a viewpoint. To understand them, and a whole trend in Soviet aesthetics, whose contribution to 'socialist realism' is crucial, it is necessary to examine the nineteenth century Russian tradition of 'revolutionary-democratic literary criticism'.

Writing of that period, Victor Erlich says:

> Since political censorship often made explicit criticism of the régime well-nigh impossible, the tasks of upholding individual rights and of exposing social evils fell largely to the creative writer. The literary artist had at his disposal numerous devices of indirection, prone to elude the watchfulness of the censor . . . The poetic parable had to be deciphered, the half-concealed idea had to be stated more explicitly, whenever the political atmosphere made possible temporarily a modicum of plain speaking. This was clearly the responsibility of the literary critic.[6]

The most important of these critics had been Herzen, Belinsky, Chernyshevsky and Dobrolyubov. They upheld what Plekhanov called the 'utilitarian' view of art, and Soviet and other Marxists found their political and materialist outlook to be the forerunners of their own. Thus Lukacs quotes approvingly from a 'deciphering' by Chernyshevsky of a love-story by Turgenev, where the critic was able to show that "the Liberals shirked the democratic tasks arising from the liberation of the serfs in the same cowardly fashion and with the same 'high-minded' excuses as Turgenev's hero, who shamefully ran away from his tryst."[7] And since this meaning contradicted Turgenev's own Liberal politics, Lukacs was able to claim the story as another example of the Engelsian 'triumph of realism' over authorial ideology.

For Chernyshevsky art had to be a textbook of life and Dobrolyubov judged a work by the extent to which it served as 'an expression of the natural aspirations of a given people or epoch.'[8] Lenin's own analyses of Tolstoy's work are very much in this tradition. In the 1908 article, 'Leo Tolstoy as a Mirror of the Russian Revolution', he showed that 'the contradictions in Tolstoy's views are indeed a mirror of those contradictory conditions in which the peasantry had to play their part in our revolution.'[9] The relationship between artistic realism and the writer's ideological position posited by Lenin differs from that implied in Engels' appreciation of Balzac. As Della Volpe (1960) pointed out, in Balzac the writing triumphs over the author's reactionary views, in effect contradicting them. But the greatness of Tolstoy's work, according to Lenin, lies in the fidelity with which it embodies the standpoint of the revolutionary peasantry, and thus the contradictions of rural Russia in the last part of the nineteenth century.

2. PROLETCULT, FORMALISM AND TROTSKY

The main thrust of Lenin's views on culture after the revolution was, however, directed in another direction. He regarded the essential task of the revolution on this front to be the attainment of mass literacy. Beside that problem, questions of art and literature were of little account. He wrote in 1923:

> At a time when we hold forth on proletarian culture and the relation in which it stands to bourgeois culture, facts and figures reveal that we are in a very bad way even as far as bourgeois culture is concerned. As might have been expected, it appears that we are still a very long way from attaining universal literacy, and that even compared with Tsarist times (1897) our progress has been far too slow. This should serve as a stern warning and reproach to those empyrean heights of 'proletarian culture'.[9]

The 'proletarian culture' at issue was the slogan of the Proletcult group headed by A. A. Bogdanov, a communist with whom Lenin had waged a bitter controversy over philosophical principles before the revolution. His position on revolutionary art was summed up in a paragraph from a resolution at the first Proletcult convention, held in 1918:

> Art by means of living images organises social experience not only in the sphere of knowledge, but also in that of the emotions and aspirations. Consequently, it is one of the most powerful implements for the organisation of collective and class forces in a class society. A class-art of its own is indispensable to the Proletariat for the organisation of its forces for social work, struggle and construction. Labour collectivism — this is the spirit of this art, which ought to reflect the world from the point of view of the labour collective, expressing the complex of its sentiment and its militant and creative will.[10]

The vast majority of the existing intelligentsia refused at first to co-operate with the Soviet State and its cultural organs. The Proletcult took full advantage of this vacuum and, partly through the encouragement of Lunacharsky, a former associate of Bogdanov, it soon had a network of 'creative writing' studios throughout the country, in which proletarians were to be trained as writers and artists.

The Proletcult refused to have any contact with intellectuals of non-proletarian origins and totally rejected the art of the past as belonging to bourgeois society. This sectarianism soon provoked a counter-attack from the Bolshevik leaders. Lenin, in any case, thought that artistic experiments must wait until the immediate tasks were accomplished. But he also felt, as did Trotsky, that in the cultural sphere the communist revolution was an *evolutionary* one: its job was to select the best from previous epochs, make it available to the masses and build upon it.

For Lenin, these were questions of strategy, based on a sense of priorities in a certain sector of social life. The intellectually agile Trotsky went further: in his *Literature and Revolution*, published in 1923, he developed a strong theoretical position on the basis of Lenin's priorities. The book took on all existing trends in Soviet letters from the standpoint of the Party which 'protects the historic interests of the working class and must be more objective and wise'.[11] On behalf of the Party, Trotsky developed theses on the nature of artistic work under socialism and on the character of art itself.

He argued that a proletarian art 'in the incomparably more weighty sense that we speak of bourgeois literature' was not possible, for two reasons. First, the general cultural level of the class was too low to provide a day-to-day milieu which would supply 'all the inspiration he [the artist] needs while at the same time mastering the procedures of his craft.' Thus the consciously proletarian writer would inevitably be reliant on the same kind of intellectual milieu as the 'fellow-travellers', the name given by Trotsky to the growing number of artists who had accepted the revolution without becoming communists. Secondly, Trotsky argued that, in theory, the notion of a specific 'proletarian culture' was incorrect. Under socialism, the role of the proletariat was to work towards the classless society, in which it would disappear along with the other classes inherited from capitalism. Only then would a 'new, real culture' develop.

In discussing the nature of artistic production, Trotsky agreed with Engels that a work's quality does not necessarily depend on its author's consciously held ideology. Thus, the 'fellow travellers' could make a contribution to Soviet literature. But, in the context of the discussion of Soviet writing directed by political beliefs of the author, the argument took a novel twist. Mayakovsky, said Trotsky, wrote powerfully, if formlessly, before aligning himself with the proletariat. But when he 'decided to swing himself round to the proletarian line, and wrote "150 Million", he suffered a most frightful rationalistic downfall. This meant that in his logic he had outrun his creative condition.'[12] In theoretical support of this analysis, Trotsky considered that the very unconscious, or non-rational character of art meant that it 'lags behind the other modes of expression of a man's spirit, and still more of the spirit of a class.'[13]

The aesthetic suggested by these various points stood in a rather perverse relation to the literary history of the early Soviet years. After his defeat by Stalin and his expulsion from the Soviet Union, it was possible for the dominant figures in cultural politics to find a Trotskyist 'deviation' in them. In fact it still is, as this definition of Trotskyism in art by Metchenko, a contemporary *apparatchik* of Soviet literary orthodoxy makes clear: '[it is] an attempt to deflect art from the ideological arena.'[14] For Trotsky's statements seemed to imply not just that a genuine political art was difficult to achieve, but to deny the possibility of an authentic artistic practice organised by a socialist ideology. It followed that even the most fervent communist artist was in reality in the same situation as a 'fellow-traveller', with no necessary link between the quality of his work and the quality of his politics.

Despite its scattered insights, *Literature and Revolution* remains a premature and sometimes superficial attempt to construct a general theory of art in a socialist society. Trotsky's impetuosity is in contrast to Lenin's more prosaic view that a proletarian literature would only be worth arguing about when there was a literate proletariat. The dominant elements of Trotsky's theory were derived from the more traditional Marxist aesthetic typified by Plekhanov. It was these which he deployed most effectively in the most celebrated section of the book, which dealt with the Formalist school of critics and poets.

The Formalists had originated in pre-Revolutionary Russia, using the recent advances in the study of linguistics to champion *avant-garde* poetry, particularly that of the Futurists. Like other *avant-garde* intellectuals, notably the Constructivists, they allied themselves with the revolution, positing a parallel between their opposition to traditional art and the rejection of traditional society by the proletariat.

However, their work provoked fervent attacks from

Marxist writers who saw their concentration on artistic forms and techniques as a denial of the social genesis and determination of a work of art. For, in its earliest phase, Formalism had polemically set itself against the 'sociological' interpretation of literature associated with Plekhanov, whose position dominated the views of orthodox Marxist critics after the Revolution.

Trotsky's was generally held to be the most effective critique of Formalism from this viewpoint, not least because he admitted that its analytical techniques were of value since art was not simply a mirror of the world, but 'a deflection, a transformation of reality in accordance with the peculiar laws of art.' Nevertheless, once these techniques were dignified by a general theoretical attempt to explain the whole of art through them, Formalism became reactionary.

> The Formalists are followers of St. John. They believe that 'in the beginning was the Word'. But we believe that in the beginning was the deed. The word followed as its phonetic shadow.[15]

Boris Eikhenbaum, a leading Formalist, replied to Trotsky by stating that Marxism and Formalism were not so much incompatible as parallel but separate endeavours, and others tried to synthesise the two into a 'formal-sociological' theory, where formalist techniques would explain the work's inner structure and Marxism would pronounce on its ideological character. But Formalism's main significance for the nascent Soviet literary theory was the challenge it posed to the idea of art as 'inspiration' or 'non-rational' (Trotsky) and its consequent psychological function (Bogdanov), which were common to all other aesthetic schools, from the Proletcult to the fellow-travellers.

Instead, the more politically committed Formalists saw themselves aligned with the more forward-looking emphasis in Soviet society, which stressed technology and the understanding of how things work. Thus, the poet Mayakovsky and the critic Osip Brik argued that the

Formalists' study of the 'laws of literary production' was 'the best educator for young proletarian writers' who are 'still afflicted with a thirst for 'self-revelation'. It will come to the aid of proletarian creative work not with hazy little chats about the "proletarian spirit" and "Communist consciousness", but with exact technical knowledge of the devices of contemporary poetic work.'[16]

The left-wing of the Formalists and Futurists set up a group and journal, LEF (Left Front of Art) to publicise their positions. One of its most important aspects was its early recognition that literature was no longer the main object of aesthetics, as those trends deriving from the nineteenth century assumed, but that the new socialist society was producing its own mass art-forms, notably the film and the graphic arts. Mayakovsky himself designed and painted posters and advertising material for state institutions, while LEF contained leading figures like the designer and typographer El Lissitsky and the film director Sergei Eisenstein.

3. THE LEFISTS AND THE SOCIAL COMMAND

El Lissitsky (1890-1941) designed the Soviet flags to be carried through Red Square on May Day in the first years of the revolution. He had taught alongside Chagall and Malevich and was heavily influenced by the ideas of Constructivism. Just as Brik and Mayakovsky politicised the main themes of Formalist theory, Lissitsky radicalised the tenets of Constructivism and put them to use in post-revolutionary society. As a movement within painting, Constructivism had provided a critique of what was called 'easel art': it opposed utilitarian criteria to traditional aesthetic values. Later, adopting new forms — posters, murals, magazines, stage-sets — Constructivist principles were brought to bear in determining the styles and uses of the new mass-media.

Lissitsky played a key role in this process, which effectively liquidated the established distinction between pure and applied art. In doing so, he brought up the question of the 'uniqueness' of the aesthetic itself, asking whether it is anything more than just one more branch of production in general. Unlike the Formalists, he posited a clear relationship between social and artistic transformations. 'The traditional book has been scattered in various directions, enlarged a hundred times, colouristically intensified and, in the form of a poster, displayed in the streets.'[17] Elsewhere, Lissitsky wrote: 'The innovation of easel-painting made great works of art possible, but it has now lost this power. The cinema and illustrated weekly have succeeded it. We rejoice in the new means which technique has put into our hands . . .'[18]

According to Lissitsky, the revolution had provided art with a new audience, 'the masses, the semi-literate masses', whose objective needs demanded new forms of communication. The LEF group used the term 'social command' (*sotsialnyy zakaz*) to describe this relationship. Osip Brik, who acted as the 'secretariat' of the group, is generally credited with originating the term. It first of all distinguished the LEF concept of the relationship between an artist and his public from preceding ones, which they felt had been made obsolete by the revolution. These included a relationship determined by 'market forces', in which an artist relied on inner compulsions to shape his work before putting it before the public in an unplanned manner, and the institutionalised system of commissions by a patron, whether aristocratic or bourgeois.

The clearest exposition of the meaning of 'social command' was in Mayakovsky's pamphlet, *How Are Verses Made?*, one of the most important pieces of literary theory to emerge from the Soviet Union in the 1920s. Too many of the writings of the controversies of the era were marred by an unproductive polemicising, which instead of sharpening the edge of an argument, merely exaggerated the points at issue. The nadir of this trend was reached after 'socialist realism' was officially installed as Party policy in 1934, and the 'police methods' of Zhdanov set the tone of cultural comment.

Mayakovsky's text is polemical — it opposes itself to the textbooks written by various literary pedants to instruct workers and peasants in the art of poetry — but the argument is presented through a detailed demonstration of the process of production of a poem. The crucial definition of social command includes the following points:

> 6. Reach for your pen only when there is no other way of saying something except verse. You must work up things you've prepared only when you feel a clear social command.
> 7. To understand the social command accurately, a poet must be in the middle of things and events. A knowledge of theoretical economics, a knowledge of the realities of everyday life, an immersion in the scientific study of history are for the poet, in the very fundamentals of his work, more important than scholarly textbooks by idealist professors who worship the past.
> 8. To fulfill the social command as well as possible you must be in the vanguard of your class, and carry on the struggle, along with your class, on all fronts. You must smash to smithereens the myth of an apolitical art. The old myth is appearing again in a new form under cover of twaddle about 'broad epic canvases' (first epic, then objective and in the end politically uncommitted) or about the 'grand style' (first grand, then elevated and in the end celestial) and so on and so forth.[19]

The distinction between this concept and the commission system is emphasised elsewhere by Mayakovsky, where he states that it would be instructive to examine 'the disparity between the social command and actual commissions'. The social command, in effect, is envisaged by Mayakovsky as the artistic equivalent of the scientific socialist politics exemplified by Lenin, an intervention of the artist into social reality.

The social command sums up the *external* relations and determinants of the production of the poem. In considering the internal factors involved, Mayakovsky uses an analogy with Marx's analysis of the process of production at the economic level: 'Poetry is a manufacture. A very difficult, very complex kind, but a manufacture.' In contrast, virtually all other Marxist aestheticians in Russia took up a reflectionist position, regarding poetry, as Lenin said of Tolstoy, as, in some sense, a *mirror* of social reality. Mayakovsky goes on to make several more points, following from his definition of it as a manufacture. A poet must start not from finished models in the past, but from understanding the 'procedures of manufacture', and 'innovation is obligatory for every poetical composition'. The importance of 'innovation' indicated Mayakovsky's adherence to the key Formalist idea of 'making strange' (*ostranie*). This term referred to the writer's ability to use artistic devices to present the familiar in an unfamiliar way, to make the reader *see* reality rather than simply recognise it. In *How Are Verses Made?* Mayakovsky was able to annex such fundamentally *avant-garde* ideas to a political theory of art, in terms which would recur in later writers, most strikingly Walter Benjamin in Germany a decade later.

The LEF artists and the theory of 'social command' came under heavy attack from the more orthodox Marxist critics. Among them was Alexander Voronsky, the communist editor of *Red Virgin Soil*, an influential journal during the early 1920s, which was closely associated with the 'fellow-travellers'. He criticised LEF for reducing art to merely a craft, and thus denying its cognitive character, its organic link with society and reflection of class relations. Voronsky, like most Marxists, saw art as possessing special characteristics (comparable, in some ways, to science) which set it apart from more mundane ideological activities. He saw, correctly, in the theories of LEF, a direct assault on such a view.

By the time Mayakovsky died in 1930, the LEF group had dissolved and its ideas had been officially censured as 'formalist', a term which carried increasing opprobrium as 'socialist realism' became the touchstone of artistic excellence. Elsewhere in Europe the ideas of the Formalist Circle were influential in more orthodox academic circles.

Mainly through the influence of the emigré Roman Jakobson, formalist methods have entered the mainstream of literary criticism through such texts as Wellek and Warren's *Theory of Literature* (Wellek and Warren, 1949). The Formalist emphasis on an immanent analysis of a text has been welcomed by an academic discipline concerned to preserve its autonomy in the face of encroachments by sociology or psychology.

In a more general sense, the Formalist stress on structural analysis has played its part in the widespread intellectual ferment of recent years termed 'structuralism'. Lévi-Strauss worked with Jakobson on a famous article which used structural linguistics to analyse Baudelaire's poem, 'Les Chats'. The 'left-wing' of structuralism has rediscovered the LEF strand of Formalist work, which has also served as something of a model for contemporary attempts to align *avant-garde* artistic work with revolutionary politics.

4. PARTY POLICIES AND THE EMERGENCE OF SOCIALIST REALISM

Throughout the 1920s, the Central Committee of the Communist Party of the Soviet Union refrained from giving official support to any particular artistic faction. The resolution of 1925, 'On The Party's Policy In The Field of Literature', stated: 'Though supervising literature as a whole, the Party can as little support any one literary fraction (classifying such fractions according to their views on form and style) as it can decide by decree the question of the form of the family.'[20]

This did not amount to a policy of *laisser-faire*, however. The Party's position on cultural issues at each stage of the first fifteen years after 1917 reflected its general, political and economic orientation, while 'supervising literature as a whole' gradually came to mean adopting certain prescriptive attitudes. The 1925 statement came during the NEP

(New Economic Policy) period and reflected the limited 'free market' situation in the economy. The limits of that freedom in literature were determined by the fact that the country had 'entered the zone of cultural revolution' and 'class warfare . . . is not coming to an end on the literary front.'

This orientation went further than Trotsky's view in *Literature and Revolution* which was not concerned with the sharp expression of class warfare in art. But it also dissociated itself from LEF by decreeing that Soviet writers should 'make use of all the technical achievements of the old masters, to work out an appropriate form, intelligible to millions.' The LEF authors, however, felt that it was the strength of their new methods that they were singularly 'intelligible to millions', especially to the 'semi-literate', as Lissitsky had put it.

The 1925 resolution provided more comfort for Voronsky's *Red Virgin Soil* group, since the heart of its argument dealt with the class relations between various group writers (proletarian, peasant, fellow-travellers) and the excesses to be avoided by proletarians in establishing hegemony over the others. This was an implicit criticism of the approach of the VAP (Association of Proletarian Writers) group, whose strict adherence to the principle of communist hegemony in literature (drawn from the Proletkult background of some of its members) had led to accusations of 'communist conceit'.

The periods of the first and second Five Year Plans saw an even greater drawing together of economic policy and artistic practice. In the first period (1928-1932), the end of NEP and the collectivisation of agriculture produced a return to the popular enthusiasm and class struggle of the immediate post-revolutionary years. Without the aid of Party decrees, the various committed artistic groups responded directly to this clear 'social command'.

LEF carried the radicalism of its theory to the logical conclusion. Following from their attack on the privileged nature of the 'aesthetic', they embarked upon a 'literature of fact', 'breaking down the distinction between writer and reader in the worker-correspondents movement' in 'a creative intervention in the realm of journalism.'[21] Thus the former stage director Tretyakov went out to factories and hydro-electric schemes to observe and describe 'socialist construction' and to participate through the editorship of wall-newspapers. For the first time LEF's work had a significant proletarian response. The Central Committee resolution 'On Measures for the Improvement of Youth and Children's Literature' (1928) also made little distinction between journalism and literature, while the new 'literature of fact' was supported by the newspaper of the Young Communists. In response to this LEF initiative RAPP (the successor to VAPP) called for 'shock workers of literature', though the results they produced were within the framework of fiction dominated by psychological realism, with clear echoes of the nineteenth-century novel. Voronsky's group opposed the 'rigidity' of both RAPP and LEF, calling for a broad socialist humanism in literature, but they were already in decline. Voronsky was expelled from the Party as a follower of Trotsky and dismissed as editor of *Red Virgin Soil*.

The Second Five Year Plan (1932-6) was constructed on the basis that the fierce class struggles were over and an era of consolidation had begun. In 1932, the consolidation of writers and artists into single unions began, with the formation of the Writers' Union. The Party decree ordering the dissolution of the rival factions was preceded by a *Pravda* editorial attacking RAPP for continuing their sectarian attitude of 'communist conceit' into an era when class conflict was in decline. Nevertheless, this criticism was at the level of literary politics, rather than policy. The approved style of Soviet literature after 1934 was based very largely on RAPP's version of a partisan psychological realism.

In 1934, Socialist Realism was officially adopted as the goal of Soviet art at the first Congress of the Writers'

Union. The keynote speeches were delivered by Gorky, Bukharin and Zhdanov, then an unknown secretary to the Central Committee. The appearance of Gorky on the platform was as important in itself as the speech he was to make. As a major pre-revolutionary realist novelist and dramatist, he embodied the link between the nineteenth-century realism of the revolutionary democrats and the new socialist version.

Gorky's contribution to the Congress was called 'Soviet Literature'. He made several disparate points. He argued that 'the bourgeoisie have never harboured any urge towards cultural creativity', a point which, despite its excellent pedigree in Marxist thought, involved his explaining the critical realism of the last century as the struggle 'against the feudal conservatism that big business had revived.' Gorky went on to call for writing which would 'make labour the principal hero of our books'. This realism was, however, to be leavened with a revolutionary romanticism. The source of this ingredient was discerned by Gorky in the potent myths which characterised the folk tale:

> If the meaning of what has been abstracted from reality is amplified through the addition of the desired and the possible — all this rounding off the image — then we have the kind of romanticism which underlies the myth, and is most beneficial in promoting a revolutionary attitude towards reality, an attitude that in practice refashions the world.[22]

Here Gorky joined a strand of Marxist thinking which emphasised art's special position by reference to its origins in tribal societies, where its function, as ritual or magic, was to encourage the 'attitude that in practice refashions the world' in the way described by Marx in the famous 1857 discussion of Greek art.

Perhaps the most intellectually distinguished intervention at a Congress whose prime object was to unify writers under the direction of the Party was that of Nikolai Bukharin (1888-1937). He had for a long time been the leading theoretician of the Soviet Party, and at this moment was temporarily 'rehabilitated' after the defeat of his right-wing group by Stalin. In the past he had differed from the prevailing Leninist line on the 'evolutionary' character of Soviet culture. In part, he held the Proletkult view that if the bourgeois State was to be smashed, so should bourgeois culture as an institutional whole. It was to be 'assimilated by the proletariat', but only 'in a different arrangement of its parts'.[23]

In his Congress speech, Bukharin contrasted art with science as a mode of cognition:

> In science, the entire qualitative diversity and uniformity of the world takes on other forms, quite distinct from immediate sensation, but giving a much more adequate reflection of reality — that is, more true . . . Art offers no abstraction from what is directly experienced. Here the sensory experience — doubly concrete and doubly 'alive' — is itself condensed.[24]

Bukharin went on to qualify this view which suggests a necessary inferiority of art to science, since art expresses only surface phenomena while science reflects the hidden 'essence' of reality. Defining art this way, he said, 'does not signify that we are dealing with an illusion or a dream . . . This essence appears in the phenomenon. The essence merges into the phenomenon. The senses do not fence us off from the world.' This final position is very close to that adopted by George Lukacs during the 1930s, in developing his own epistemology of socialist realism.

Bukharin did not further develop this point, however, but turned to consider the material of literary art, the word. Like Trotsky a decade earlier, he directly acknowledged the technical expertise of the Formalists, and called for a sociological analysis of language. In doing so his approach converged with that of a significant but often neglected trend in Formalist linguistics, associated with the work of Mikhail Bakhtin (who also wrote under the name V. N. Volosinov).[25] Bakhtin had tried to construct a Marxist theory of language by regarding the word as 'the ideological phenomenon *par excellence*' and allying himself with the new Soviet psychology of Pavlov and Vygotsky. In doing so, he attempted to transcend the deadlock between the asocial systematisation of language by the Formalists, and the reliance on a vague notion of 'social psychology' derived from Plekhanov which served orthodox Marxism as a link between social base and linguistic construct. Language itself was the product of history and class struggle, and in Bukharin's phrase, 'Within the microcosm of the word is embedded the macrocosm of history'.

The contribution of Bukharin to the definition of the new model of Soviet writing took an historical form. He pointed to the long history of the social function of art, beginning with 'the ancient cosmogonies which were veritable encyclopedias', while the study of literature in Rome was the means whereby:

> The society and the social leaders were reproducing themselves in the realm of ideas, in an idealised form, inculcating their ideas, thoughts, conceptions, feelings, characters, ambitions, ideals, virtues.[26]

Both these elements, perhaps surprisingly, were to become important aspects of the practice of socialist realism in fiction. The integration of technological and scientific detail into the text gave the novel the function of a 'poetical encyclopedia', while the Roman reproduction of the values of the society through literature was central to the partisan character of socialist realism and such aspects as its 'positive hero', although not always in accordance with Bukharin's warning that: 'unity does not mean that we must all sing the same song at the same time . . . Unity does not mean the presentation of the same ideal types and 'villains', nor the abolition on paper of all contradictions and evils.'[27]

In its original formulation, socialist realism was not a uniform style, but a single perspective or viewpoint all writers were to adopt. The perspective was determined by the nature of Soviet society, and by the new audience it offered to the writer. This constant theme in Soviet literary debate was reiterated by Bukharin, at the Congress:

> In the socialist society which is coming into being, the difference between physical labour and brainwork is gradually being replaced. A new type of man is arising who knows the world in order to change it. Mere contemplation, mere portrayal of the objective, without elucidation of the motive tendencies, without reference to the practical alteration of the objective world, are here receding into the past. Hence socialist realism cannot base its views on the naturalism of Zola, who proposed to describe reality 'such as it is' and nothing more. Neither can it accept his other slogan, 'imagination is no longer needed'. Socialist realism dares to 'dream' and should do so, basing itself on the real trends of development.[28]

The exhortatory tone of this is the authentic tone of socialist realism as an administrative fiat. The attack on naturalism is a common theme, to be developed most fully by Lukacs, while the uneasy 'scientific utopianism' of the last sentence is indicative of the Party's suspicion of the artistic licence suggested by allowing the writer to 'dream'. The relationship posed between a new kind of art and the abolition of the division of labour within Soviet society is peculiar to Bukharin, but its theoretical interest is reduced when it is realised that the 1930s saw the beginning of an increasing stratification of Soviet society, with the intelligentsia sharply distinguished from the working class. The era of Tretyakov's 'worker correspondents' was over and the solidification of artists into a caste was signalled by the formation of the Writers, Painters, Film Workers and Composers Unions, expulsion from which effectively meant the end of an artist's career.

The administrator of socialist realism *par excellence* was A. A. Zhdanov (1896-1948) whose keynote speech at the first Writer's Congress marked the beginning of his domination of Soviet cultural life. He began by outlining the political situation after the recent 17th Party Congress. It was necessary 'to eradicate the vestiges of capitalism in our economy and in people's minds'. Zhdanov's own rudimentary aesthetic was a combination of a Plekhanovite sociology of art, in which the work reflected the society which produced it, with a voluntaristic directive to artists to produce such literature. Thus, just as Soviet literature 'reflects the successes and achievements of the socialist system', so 'the decline and decay of bourgeois literature derive from the decline and decay of the capitalist system'. The Soviet writer must consider Stalin's description of him as an 'engineer of the human soul', and consider what obligation such a role put on him. Zhdanov obligingly answered the question, in an influential definition of socialist realism:

> It means, in the first place, that you must know life in order to be able to depict it truthfully in artistic creations, to depict it neither 'scholastically' nor lifelessly, not simply as 'objective reality', but rather as reality in its revolutionary development. The truthfulness and historical exactitude of the artistic image must be linked with the task of ideological transformation, of the education of the working people in the spirit of socialism. This method in fiction and literary criticism is what we call the method of socialist realism.[29]

Although Zdhanov agreed with Bukharin that this 'method' did not prescribe a style for socialist realist works ('You have many weapons at your disposal'), a dominant style soon emerged as the first masterpieces of the new method were hailed. Among them were Fadeyev's *Chapayev* (1932) and Ostrovsky's *How The Steel Was Tempered* (1934). Both were autobiographical novels of psychological realism and both contributed significantly to the model of the 'positive hero' in Soviet fiction. Ostrovsky's book went on to sell over forty million copies and the idealism of its central figure in his devotion to the Party was held up for emulation to successive generations of young communists.

As Brewster (1976), puts it, the theoretical tenets of socialist realism drew on the various strands of aesthetic thought in the 1920s, and the theory was, to some extent, as much a product of those struggles as something imposed on writers by the Party from outside: 'The central demand for an intuitive realism obviously appealed to Pereval (the *Red Virgin Soil* group), while the inclusion of revolutionary romanticism leans more towards the Proletkult and the phrase 'engineers of the human soul' has a distinctly leftist ring.'

Yet, in practice, socialist realism came to mean the adoption of the techniques of nineteenth century realist fiction and painting and their combination with a new socialist content. The model in painting was Repin, the democratic artist of the Tsarist era. In literature, the heroes were Tolstoy and Gorky. In the cinema, the experimental work of Eisenstein, Pudovkin and Vertov during the 1920s was abandoned in favour of a style mirroring the narrative movement of the realist novel.[30] Most full-length films of the 1930s were treatments of already successful novels, such as *Chapayev*, or of officially sanctioned historical themes: the last film completed by Eisenstein dealt with the national hero Alexander Nevsky, a project undertaken at the behest of Stalin himself. His *Bezhin Meadow* was ordered to be curtailed during shooting because Eisenstein's 'revolutionary romanticism' was too revolutionary for the authorities, while his plan to make a film of Marx's *Capital* was never to be realised. In music, the new orthodoxy took longer to formulate. As an art form it had a lower priority from the point of view of 'ideological transformation' (the first Congress of Composers took place only in 1948), and there were problems in defining a musical socialist realism. In the event the use of 'decadent' ideas from Western modern music was used as a negative touchstone with which to assail Shostakovitch and others as 'formalists'.

'Formalism' was the primary deviation an artist could be guilty of in the Zhdanovite era. If it had any precise meaning, it signified an unwillingness to utilise the officially-sanctioned artistic forms and an 'unhealthy' interest in methods in use among the *avant-garde* in capitalist countries, which were necessarily contaminated by the decay of that social system. There was a logical problem for socialist realism when it came to the question of the 'progressive realist' artists of capitalist countries ('critical realists' in Lukacs' terminology), particularly when the Comintern adopted the Popular Front policy of co-operation with other anti-Fascist parties. But since the concept of socialist realism was never a systematic one, use could be made of the old 'triumph of realism' idea, so that these bourgeois artists escaped the fate of their decadent colleagues by adopting the right artistic method (classical realism) and also by their friendship for the USSR, a less exact criterion which brought such an unlikely figure as André Gide into the ranks of the progressive writers.

5. THE EVOLUTION OF SOCIALIST REALISM

The *political* history of artistic production and publication in the Soviet Union since 1934 is tortuous and complex. In contrast, there is little history of aesthetic theory, almost none of theoretical debate. The Soviet cultural institutions involve a division of labour between critics and scholars. The former act as ideological commentators on the immediate issues, while the latter are historical researchers. Since the beginnings of 'de-Stalinisation' in 1956, certain reformulations of socialist realist theory have occurred, to the extent of widening the stylistic limits within which its methods can be authentically applied. Thus, Brecht is now admitted to the pantheon, when in the 1930s he was suspected of being tainted with 'modernism'.

Amongst scholars, a certain amount of work has been undertaken to provide socialist realism with a more firmly founded Marxist pedigree. Lifshitz's volume on Marx's aesthetic thought attempted to find in the early works the basis for a Marxist theory of art independent of the nineteenth century realist tradition. Following him, Yuri Davidov (1967) has reformulated the history of Soviet

aesthetics in the 1920s by positively evaluating Mayakovsky and the symbolist poet Blok in the light of an
'early Marxist' aesthetic. He distinguishes these writers
from the 'ultra-left' trends of the period who, according to
Davidov, made the fatal mistake of denying the specificity
of art as a social practice. In doing so, he treats at length the
theories of the LEF group as well as the ideas of Boris
Arvatov, who founded a theory of art as production. But
perhaps the most significant revision of official theory in
Davidov's work is his attack on the ideas of the later
Tolstoy, whom he accuses of a 'primitive communist' view
of art, referring to Tolstoy's statement that art in its present
form should be abolished.

The period of 'the thaw' under Khruschev found certain
Western communist writers undertaking a more radical re-
appraisal of the tenets of socialist realism. The most influential of these were Roger Garaudy (1963) and Ernst
Fischer (1963). The critique implied by Garaudy's 'realism
without boundaries' and Fischer's 'socialist art' centred on
the orthodox Soviet condemnation of 'modernism' and
'decadence'. The work of Franz Kafka became a crucial
area over which the battle was waged, not least because of
the emergence of 'revisionist' Marxists within communist
Czechoslovakia, who wished to claim Kafka as part of their
national radical heritage.[32]

The debate was in many ways unsatisfactory. The old
guard Russian critics stubbornly maintained that anything
which was pessimistic and which 'distorted' the novel of
psychological realism was anti-humanist. Garaudy, Fischer
and others had recourse to the theory of alienation, arguing
that the alienation of the individual was a central feature of
modern capitalism and that Kafka, Beckett and the other
modernists had the virtue of expressing alienation with
depth and intensity. The old guard replied that alienation
was an effect of private property, something which Kafka
did not understand. Therefore, in his books, 'the irrational
takes the place of a true understanding of objective

reality.'[31] At a deeper theoretical level, what was under attack was the foundation of socialist realism in a concept of the *reflection* of reality. For orthodox socialist realism, Kafka and Picasso cannot be admitted to the canon, whatever progressive views are claimed for their work, because they have transgressed against the principle of reflection and hence cannot produce genuine knowledge of the external world. Such a view is at the heart of the most sustained and weighty attempt to provide socialist realism with a theoretical apparatus, that of the Hungarian philosopher Georg Lukacs.[33]

BIBLIOGRAPHICAL NOTE

Brewster (1976) provides a brief chronology of the 1917-34 period, to which my own account is indebted. Many other studies of this phase focus on the literature and art, regarding the political aspect as unfortunately relevant. However, some studies of particular movements and institutions are recommended, particularly Fitzpatrick (1970), Brown (1953), Erlich (1965) and Vaughan James (1973).

Lenin's aesthetics receive contrasting interpretations from Macherey (1966) and Lukacs (1950). The links with the nineteenth-century revolutionary democrats are summarised in Vaughan James (1973). For translations of Formalist texts, see Todorov (1965) and Brik (1974). Lissitsky's work is discussed in Bojko (1972), while an unusual intellectual biography of Mayakovsky is provided by Shlovsky (1975). Bakhtin's importance as a critic is underlined in Kristeva (1972).

Chapter Three

THE GERMAN DEBATES

1. LUKACS' REALISM

UNTIL the success of the Russian Revolution, the largest and most prestigious Marxist organisation had been the German Social Democratic Party. In addition to its trade union and (electoral) political activities, it had a flourishing cultural life. Literary questions had been debated at its national congress, and its leading intellectuals (Kautsky, Bebel and above all Franz Mehring) commented on cultural and artistic matters for the flourishing Party press.

The tradition was carried on by the Communist Party of Germany, formed after the abortive 1919 Revolution and the proclamation of the Third International. Its cultural strength was increased by the radicalisation of significant numbers of the intelligentsia in response to the economic decline and political impotence of the Weimer Republic. Among the leading left artists in the decade prior to Hitler's coming to power in 1933 were: George Grosz, John Heartfield (graphic arts, photomontage); Erwin Piscator, Bertolt Brecht (theatre); Hanns Eisler, Kurt Weill (music); Lion Feuchtwangler, Anna Seghers, Johannes Becher (literature).

In 1928, the Communist Party was instrumental in setting up a "League of Proletarian Revolutionary Writers" to co-ordinate left activity in the arts. Within the League an important debate on the correct nature of revolutionary art took place, whose implications would be far-reaching for Marxist aesthetics in general.

At the outset, the terms of the debate owed much to the disputes in Soviet literary circles in the late 1920s. The key term was 'realism' and the leading group in the League fought for their definition of the term through an attack on authors seen to have deviated from that norm. The principal protagonist was the Hungarian, Georg Lukacs (1886-1971). In 1931 he arrived in Berlin from Moscow, where he had worked with Lifshitz and others on Marx and Engels' writings on art. Using Engels' appreciation of Balzac and Lenin's articles on Tolstoy, Lukacs used the principles underlying the classical realist novel as a touchstone for his critiques of the 'naturalism' and 'expressionism' he discerned in the work of left-wing German writers. The concept of realism espoused by Lukacs anticipated the theory of socialist realism in important respects.

This was a turning-point in his long political and intellectual career. Before turning to Marxism as a result of the Russian Revolution and the short-lived Hungarian Soviet Republic of 1919 (in which he was Commissar for Education), Lukacs had established a reputation as an aesthetician with *The Soul and Forms* (1910) and the Hegelian *Theory of the Novel* (1971a), originally written in 1916. His subsequent career as a political theorist was stormy and brief. He published the famous collection of essays *History and Class Consciousness* in 1923 and aligned himself with the 'Kommunismus' group, a left-wing tendency in German communism. They called for 'partial insurrections' as a tactic to 'overcome the ideological crisis and Menshevik lethargy of the proletariat and standstill of revolutionary development'. The results of these shock tactics were disastrous and Lukacs himself, in the uncertain political climate of international communism at the end of the 1920s, undertook a retreat into the less turbulent waters of aesthetics, after publishing an impeccably orthodox study of Lenin's politics.

Later, as an exile in Moscow from 1933 to 1945 and thereafter as a professor in Budapest, Lukacs produced a stream of theoretical and critical studies, mainly devoted to the novel and its tradition. But the German situation of the early 1930s found him working out his basic theory in terms of day-to-day arguments over particular works and trends. With his German allies, Lukacs translated the RAPPist attack on LEF into the Berlin cultural milieu.

The artistic techniques attacked by Lukacs included reportage, montage and the episodic construction of works. These elements were particularly apparent in the novels of Ottwald and Doblin and the plays of Brecht. Doblin was a doctor whose novels and stories were associated with the Expressionist movement and who was clearly influenced by the episodic construction of John Dos Passos, with his montage of heterogeneous elements designed to convey the complexity of city life. The contemporary author Gunter Grass has acknowledged Ottwald as a major influence. Ottwald was the author of a documentary novel, *For they know not what they are doing. A novel about German justice*, which was the object of a scathing attack by Lukacs in *Linkscurbe*, the League's journal, in 1932. Brecht was undoubtedly the most important of Lukacs' antagonists but at this stage was not attacked directly. Instead, his work was condemned by association with the 'expressionism' of Doblin and others.

There seems little doubt that Lukacs was carrying out a parallel policy to that of the Moscow 'realists', to rid the cultural left of 'deviationists'. References to 'literary Trotskyism' turn up in the writings of this period. But at the theoretical level Lukacs' view of what constituted 'decadence' in art and its identification with 'modernism' coincided with that of the Soviet critics. For both parties the principles of socialist writing were rooted in the method of nineteenth-century classic fiction, although there was some difference of emphasis when the differences between 'socialist' and 'critical' realism were discussed. Lukacs was frequently criticised for not appearing to want there to be any difference save that of subject-matter. He regarded the fully successful work of art as one which provides:

> . . . an image of reality in which the oppositions of appearance and

essence, of the individual case and the general rule, of the immediacy of the senses and abstract conceptualisation etc., are resolved. The immediate effect of the work of art is to dissolve the oppositional elements into a spontaneous whole, so that they form an inseparable unity for the reader.[1]

Like Bukharin, Lukacs saw the particular role of art as the uniting of the various opposing aspects of reality, the abstract and the concrete, into a 'spontaneous whole' through which the reader immediately absorbs both the phenomenal forms of the world and their inner meaning. The special form which enables this to be achieved is, for Lukacs, the *intensive totality* of the art-work. This intensive totality is the reflection in artistic form of the extensive totality of reality, through a process of selection of the essential and the typical. In this way, Lukacs' theory avoids the twin errors of naturalism and expressionism. To reproduce merely the appearance of things is to be naturalistic, while formalism, expressionism, the montage theory, result from an attempt to grasp only the essence of things, ignoring their recognisable appearances. To choose such incorrect methods was, in effect, to become a victim of contemporary bourgeois society. For through such processes as 'alienation' and 'reification', that society acted to fragment the world of the individual. The expressionists and naturalistic writers merely reproduced this fragmentation, while the truly realist writer could overcome it.

This argument, already more coherent than the majority of Soviet theories of the 1920s, is only one part of the vast theoretical edifice erected by Lukacs in over half a century of writing. The nature of his enterprise has been summed up by Lichtheim (1970): '. . . a theory of aesthetics which would do for the new world of East European socialism what German idealism in general, and Hegel in particular, had done for the bourgeois world. If . . . he has not become "the Marx of aesthetics", it is at least arguable that he has done for his chosen topic what Dilthey did for Kant and Hegel: he has systematised a body of ideas that was once novel and revolutionary, and thus rendered it fit for academic consumption.' It should be added that Lichtheim's conclusion is probably too sweeping. While Lukacs' aim was indeed to produce a system of Marxist aesthetics, the problematic nature of artistic and philosophical practice in 'the new world of East European socialism' has frequently meant that the 'academic' and the political are closely linked.

The scope of Lukacs' project was therefore ambitious: an attempt to produce a Marxist aesthetics, fully underpinned by a coherent philosophical and theoretical position. But what is immediately striking about his work is the contrast between the grandeur of that aim and the very narrow sector of artistic production upon which it is based. Drama, poetry, painting, sculpture, music and film receive little or no attention in the Lukacs *oeuvre*. The focus is constantly on the novel, or more specifically on *narrative*, a concept which Jameson (1971) argues persuasively is central to Lukacs' theory.

The term describes certain common features of the epic and the novel, the genres which figured largely in the *Theory Of The Novel*. This work attempted an ambitious periodisation of cultural history, in parallel with history in general. The ideal type of artistic form is the Greek epic, which is truly *concrete*, a term which assumes great positive value throughout Lukacs' work, even though its content varies. In Jameson's paraphrase, epic narration:

> . . . is only possible when daily life is still felt to be meaningful and immediately comprehensible down to its smallest details. After this utopia, in which essence and life are one, the two terms begin to fall apart and the place of epic is taken by tragedy.[2]

Tragic drama and Platonic idealist philosophy are shown by Lukacs to be modes of disintegration of the truly concrete, but the novel form is an attempt 'to recapture something of the quality of epic narration as a reconciliation between matter and spirit, between life and essence.'[3] The 'form' of the novel, thus takes on a greater significance in the *Theory Of The Novel* than the conventional definition of the husk surrounding the content of a work would indicate.

In a self-criticism, part of a new introduction to the book written in 1962, Lukacs described its mode of procedure in this way:

> It became the fashion to start off from a few characteristic traits of the tendency or period — traits usually grasped in a purely intuitive fashion — then to synthesise general concepts from them, and finally to return deductively to individual phenomena, in the conviction that this amounted to a grandiose view of the totality.[4]

But in criticising his methodology in the book, Lukacs does not directly attack the Hegelian thesis it embodied, notably the cyclical idea of the recovery of a lost (Greek) harmony. In the new introduction he referred to the work as one in which 'Hegelian philosophy was concretely applied to aesthetic problems'. The continuity of Lukacs' work on aesthetics could be described by saying that he retained this general approach in his later writings, notably the value placed on the novel as a *form*, although the Hegelian philosophy was replaced by a Marxist one, albeit a Marxism which still owed much to Hegel. The point is even clearer in relation to the most important of Lukacs' disciples, Lucien Goldmann, whose codification of Lukacsian ideas into a somewhat rigid historical schema makes obvious the debt to Hegel.

There is not space here to do full justice to the complexities of Lukacs' intellectual heritage or his political career. His aesthetics, however, are anchored in an analysis of capitalist society which derives ultimately from his 1923 text, *History and Class Consciousness*, an analysis which makes it clear why it is only the realist novel form which can adequately portray that society in artistic terms. Condemned as heretical by the communist orthodoxy at the time, *History and Class Consciousness* was later repudiated by its author, but it is remarkable how much of Lukacs' specifically literary analysis remained dependent on certain of its theses.

From his earliest to his last writings, Lukacs considered capitalism to be in principle inimical to great art. He had an important precedent for this view in Marx's early writings, although as Stedman Jones (1971) pointed out, the dichotomy between industrialism and nature (including human nature) was a general nineteenth-century theme. Lukacs' argument, however, was far removed from the romanticism or anti-rationalism of other attacks on industrial capitalism.

He developed the concept of the fetishism of commodities to be found in *Capital* into a general theory of consciousness and ideology. Thus, the determining factor in human consciousness within capitalism was the commodity form, in which the exchange-value of the products of human labour dominated their use-values. From this flowed the twin processes of alienation and reification, as a result of which men lived in a mystified relationship to their products and to each other. Social relationships were seen as relations between things, not people, and men's products were experienced as something alien to them. Additionally, the division of labour resulted not only in specialisation but the fragmentation of experience and thought, destroying 'every image of the Whole'.

The conditions of existence for people living under capitalism therefore constituted a block to their forming a total view of the world. At this point Lukacs had reached by a Marxist route the same conclusion as in the *Theory Of The Novel*: in the modern world everyday life was 'opaque' and separated from meaningfulness. Lukacs then had to make a further move in order to satisfy the philosophical demand that his theory should explain its own existence in a society apparently condemned to the fragmentation of thought. This knowledge of the truth of capitalism, he argued, was impossible for bourgeois thought, since to attain such self-knowledge would mean a realisation of its necessary abolition as a class. But the proletariat, which experiences reification and alienation to the full is so placed that *its* self-knowledge (which is Marxism) would mean an awareness of its potential for liberation through the abolition of capitalism. The similarity in Lukacs' early theory between the developing self-knowledge of humanity through a series of class societies, and the unfolding of Hegel's 'Absolute Spirit' has been criticised by many orthodox Marxist opponents of Lukacs.

Lukacs himself claimed that, in important ways, his later writings on aesthetics did break with the presuppositions of *History and Class Consciousness*, notably in the more specific historical basis of his judgements and the introduction of the relation of class forces (class struggle) as a key determinant of superstructural (artistic) practice. Yet there was also a continuity, in the criteria of excellence applied in judging realist art, and in a remaining tendency to a sweeping periodisation.

Perhaps the text in which all these elements are to be found in a most characteristic amalgam is *The Historical Novel* (1962). Dismissed by Lichtheim as "middle-brow", the book is in fact extremely impressive in its combination of a consistent theoretical framework with detailed reference to a vast number of novelists. For Lukacs, the category 'historical novel' tends to come to mean great novel, the one that can treat its subject matter, contemporary or not, in a fully historical manner.

According to this work, 1848 marked the high point not only of the revolutionary wave throughout Europe, but also of the historical novel. In another essay written at the same period, Lukacs put the matter in a more perfunctory way:

> The defeat of the 1848 uprisings in the most important Western European countries and in England the collapse of Chartism brought about a profound general ideological depression. This turning-point in historical development is mirrored in literature . . . A universal despairing pessimism descends on the greatest writers and in the tragic figures of Flaubert and Baudelaire this pessimism degenerates into nihilism . . . (The atmosphere of gloom in Dickens' later writings is also a product of this period).[5]

This is Lukacs at his least engaging. The oversimplification is in part a product of his writing for a Soviet audience in the 1930s, yet the tone of dogmatic insistence was also part of his polemical armoury, to be used against the hapless Ottwald as well as Kafka and Sartre.

The Historical Novel develops the 1848 thesis in more detail. The heroic age of the novel, before the defeats of that crucial year, is linked to the mobilisation of the masses in the period of the Revolutionary Wars. The armies of Napoleon and his enemies were the first modern popular armies, in which the participating masses could see themselves making history, even if they were under the direction of their rulers. In this atmosphere, the historical novel — the book which lays out the full panorama of the society — could flourish. But, with the defeats of 1848, the bourgeoisie, which had formally led the popular classes, was no longer progressive. It now proceeded to establish itself as a ruling class and to expand industrial capitalism.

For Lukacs, then, the determining factor in the literary potential of an age, of the character and quality of the work produced, is the *political* role of a class. However, the continuing economic characteristics of the era — the commodity form and consequent fragmentation of life — determine the artistic means by which the era can be 'reflected'. The Lukacsian history of Western European writing sees the next phase (1848 to approximately 1880) as one of decline and failure, of naturalism (Zola is one of the favourite whipping-boys) and escapism or decadence. The following epoch finds the emergence of Imperialism and Fascism producing in opposition a generation of artists opposed to the 'privatisation' of their predecessors (Shaw, Ibsen) and then the 'democratic humanists' whose 'historical novel reflects the main anti-barbaric tendencies possible under dying capitalism, [and] also reveals the growing ideological influence which the socialist humanism of the Soviet Union has exercised upon the best intellectuals of the West.'[6]

Written in 1937, this quotation encapsulates Lukacs' final position as a critic of contemporary writing: the objective possibilities of a renewal of the values of great art (which means the 'realism' of Greek epic and classic novel) are present in twin humanisms of the 'democrats' of the West (notably Thomas Mann) and the socialism of the Soviet Union. The political parallels to this aesthetic situation are cited by Lukacs directly in his later works: the Popular Front of progressive forces in the 1930s, and the struggle for 'peaceful co-existence' in the post-war era.

Lukacs' work also includes explorations of the ontology of art, and an approach to the problem of the origin of the aesthetic in human labour.[7] But in order to show his ideas in action, as a guide to the production of a socialist art, it is necessary to return to his debate with the playwright and author Bertolt Brecht during the 1930s.

2. BRECHT AGAINST LUKACS

The debate itself was an indirect one. Lukacs' attacks on current literary practice hardly mentioned Brecht by name, while the dramatist's response, a series of articles written in 1938, remained unpublished until 1967, a decade after his death (Brecht, 1974). Their main emphasis is on the inadequacy of Lukacs' ideas as a theory which might guide or inform the practice of a contemporary committed writer.

The criticism is, in part, that of a producer of art directed against a consumer who, as a critic, attempts to formulate rules of the right and wrong way to produce art. But Lukacs was not just an ordinary critic. With his colleagues on the editorial board of *Das Wort*, the emigré cultural journal published in Moscow, he enjoyed a privileged position within Soviet intellectual life, which implied an access to power as well as prestige. While working on the anti-critique of Lukacs, Brecht said of him and his allies:

> They are, to put it bluntly, enemies of production. Production makes them uncomfortable. You never know where you are with production. Production is the unforeseeable. You never know what's going to come out. And they themselves don't want to

produce. They want to play the apparatchik and exercise control over other people. Every one of their criticisms contains a threat.[8]

For Brecht, the advice to writers offered by Lukacs came down to: 'Be like Tolstoy — but without his weaknesses! Be like Balzac — only up-to-date!' This criticism was made from the point of view of the theorist as well as the producer. Brecht reversed the terms of the argument by accusing Lukacs of being the real 'formalist'. The attack centred on the rigidity of the models held up by Lukacs to socialist authors for emulation. They were drawn from the novel, without reference to drama or poetry (the two fields which most preoccupied Brecht himself); they were purely literary, implicitly denying the importance of contemporary political and social developments in determining a writer's choice of form or style; and they overlooked the fact that, from a Marxist perspective, the portrayal of character in the 'classic' novel must itself have been conditioned by the limits of its historical situation:

> No, Balzac does not indulge in montage. But he writes vast genea-logies, he marries off the creatures of his fantasy as Napoleon did his marshals and brothers; he follows possessions (fetishism of objects) through generations of families and their transference from one to the other. He deals with nothing but the 'organic': families are organisms in which the organisms grow.[9]

Such an approach, eminently suitable to portray the bourgeois family in all its plenitude, is, Brecht argues, equally unsuitable when it is the working-class family (Brecht's *The Mother*) or familial relations under socialism (*The Caucasian Chalk Circle*) that is in question. There, the organic must be replaced by the social, the unchanging by the changeable. Brecht amplifies the point by offering an alternative definition of realism to that of Lukacs:

> We shall not speak of a realistic manner of writing only when for example, we can smell, taste and feel 'everything', when there is 'atmosphere' and when plots are so contrived that they lead to psy-chological analysis of character. Our concept of realism must be wide and political, sovereign over all conventions. Realistic means: discovering the causal complexes of society/unmasking the prevailing view of things as the view of those who rule it/writ-

ing from the standpoint of the class which offers the broadest solutions for the pressing difficulties in which human society is caught/emphasising the element of development/making possible the concrete, and making possible abstraction from it.[10]

The scope of this definition emphasises the fact that Brecht's theories of art and its functioning are far more than an apologia for his practice of theatre and its innovations. That is, however, how he has been generally regard in Western Europe and North America since the 1950s. In fact, Brecht's body of work represents the first authentic combination of theory and practice by a Marxist in the field of the arts. As such, it represents a difficulty for the traditional division of labour between the 'spontaneous' artist and the reflective theorist.

This was first recognised in 1956 by the French writer Roland Barthes, who analysed the variety of responses to Brecht's plays on their performance in Paris by his Berliner Ensemble. For the liberal Right,

> Brecht is the object of a traditional exercise in political neutralisation: the man is separated from the work and the first is abandoned to politics . . . while the second is recruited to the ranks of the Eternal Theatre: the work of Brecht, they say, is great in spite of the man, against him.[11]

On the left, writes Barthes, are those who regard Brecht as a great humanist artist, alongside Thomas Mann or Romain Rolland, again ignoring the systematic ("non-creative") side of his work, and expressing "an anti-intellectual prejudice, common in certain parts of the extreme left'. There are also the 'Zhdanovites' who attack Brecht for his 'opposition to the positive hero, his notion of epic theatre and the formalist orientation of his plays'. This is also the main direction of Lukacs' critique.

The criticism referred to by Barthes concerns Brecht's 'epic theatre', a dramatic mode which he adopted in order to 'unmask the prevailing view of things', which he felt was upheld by the 'Aristotelean' drama of the day. Born in 1898, he wrote his first plays during the 1920s; in Berlin during the Weimar years the expressionism of these early works gave way to a radically new theatre as his political commitment deepened. The plays of this phase included *The Threepenny Opera*, *The Mother* (an adaptation of Gorky's novel) and *A Man's a Man*. He also collaborated with Ottwald on a film, *Kuhle Wampe*. Brecht went into exile from 1933 to 1947, living and working in Denmark, Sweden, Finland and the USA. *Mother Courage*, *The Caucasian Chalk Circle* and *Galileo* were written during these years. In 1947 he returned to East Germany, where he directed the Berliner Ensemble with his wife, the actress Helene Weigel. During his career he wrote hundreds of poems, as well as essays, reviews and fragments on all aspects of art and aesthetics. He died in 1956.

Since that time, and in particular since the publication of the collected works in Germany during the 1960s, Marxist commentators on Brecht have been able to place the specifics of his new theory of drama in a more general aesthetic context, and have found in them the basis for an alternative position to that of orthodox socialist realism. The ideas of 'epic theatre' thus become one aspect of an overall theory.

Nevertheless, 'epic theatre' marks the point at which Brecht's practice and theory coincide most forcibly. In an early attempt at its definition, he counterposed a list of its features with those of the traditional Aristotelean 'dramatic theatre'. While the latter implicates the spectator in the situation of the characters, epic theatre 'turns the spectator into an observer but . . . arouses his capacity for action'. Where dramatic theatre 'provides him with sensations', epic theatre 'forces him to take decisions'. In the tragic drama of the former, 'man is unalterable'; in the episodic narrative of epic theatre, 'he is alterable and able to alter'.

The fundamental argument is that dramatic theatre reinforces the passivity of the audience, ensuring their reconciliation with the world as it is. Two of the most important mechanisms for this are 'empathy', the total identification of the spectator with a character, and 'catharsis', Aristotle's description of the purging of the audience of their emotions of pity and fear in the dramatic climax of tragedy. To these mechanisms Brecht opposed a method of characterisation by which the actor would *present* the character to the audience so that they could regard his or her behaviour in an objective fashion, and he proposed an open ending to the play, so that the conclusion could be sought by the audience in the world outside. 'Catharsis' merely acted to discourage any such action, by providing an 'organic' ending to the play, thus sealing it off from contact with the outside world.

Solomon (1974) takes issue with Brecht's attack on catharsis, arguing that it is progressive because it can 'purge the violent and anti-human drives of man' and its 'symbolic solutions within the theatre (the happy ending, reconciliation, "recognition" in the Aristotelean sense) serves as models of a release which the audience will seek in reality (politically) if the social-historical factors are favourable.'[12] Without saying what these favourable factors would be, Solomon goes beyond Lukacs in discussing the effects of a work of art, an element which is not logically necessary to the theory of the 'intensive totality'. He differs from both Brecht and Lukacs in granting primacy to feeling over reason in aesthetic experience, and asserts that the *mimetic* nature of traditional drama, its modelling of reality, can itself provoke political action.

The critique of Brecht seems to rely on a timeless idea of the organisation of the emotions and their relationship to art: are 'the violent . . . drives of man' always 'anti-human'? Brecht's theory, however, is based on a definition of the political character of the present era. Within the epoch of the decline of capitalist society, art's main task, according to Brecht, is to assist the masses in becoming the subject rather than the object of history. Art can do this by encouraging their active participation in the world, by providing an occasion for the thinking about the world that is necessary to change it. In addition to evoking the emotions which connote class *solidarity*, the theatre can help to develop the habits of critical thought which go to make up class political *consciousness*.

It is in this perspective that the attack on the cathartic ending becomes significant. Gallas (1973) writes that:

> For Brecht, totality is only reached in the process of reception, it is not represented solely by the work of art as such. The work itself is 'open', still 'incomplete'. The spectator either engages with Brecht's method and draws the conclusion independently, or the whole point of the performance will escape him, he 'gains nothing' from it, he 'takes nothing away with him'.[13]

In contrast, the Lukacsian totality is completed by the artist. The 'many-sided' characters of the novels of both critical and socialist realism ('the positive hero') provide in themselves an alternative to the fragmentation of daily life (in capitalist countries) or a model for emulation (within socialism).

3. BENJAMIN, ADORNO, AND CRITICAL THEORY

The recent use of Brecht as a general theorist viewing art as a form of production, rather than one of expression or reflection, has been strongly influenced by the writings of the critic and essayist Walter Benjamin (1892-1940), whose work on Brecht is collected in the volume *Understanding Brecht* (Benjamin, 1973). In addition to the specific articles expounding the key concepts of Brechtian theatre and poetry, Benjamin generalised Brecht's position in his essay, 'The Author as Producer'.

The starting point for this talk, delivered in Paris in 1934, was the unproductive argument within Marxist aesthetics about the relationship in the work of committed artists, of 'form' and 'content' (Benjamin employs the more exact terms, 'quality' and 'tendency'). The frequent resolution of the argument was with the statement that both are necessary because art that is politically correct can only be effective if it is of a high quality. However, said Benjamin, to understand the implications of that essentially correct solution for the practice of art, the 'literary relations of production' must be examined. This view is opposed to the sociological perspective in which what matters is only the writer's position in regard to the relations of production in general, the relations between capital and labour.

Unless this new position is adopted, Benjamin argued, the situation of the committed writer will be like those German radicals of the Weimar period who 'underwent a revolutionary development in terms of their *mentality* — without at the same time being able to think through in a really revolutionary way the question of their own work, its relationship to the means of production and its technique'.[14] By refining the given techniques and choosing politically significant subject matter, 'left-wing' photography succeeds only 'in turning abject poverty itself, by handling it in a modish, technically perfect way, into an object of enjoyment'. Instead, Benjamin points to the practice of photo-montage (Grosz and Heartfield) and to the need for the photographer to put such 'a caption beneath his picture as will rescue it from the ravages of modishness and confer upon it a revolutionary use value'.[15]

The revolutionary artist, therefore, must not simply utilise the means of artistic production in the way they are employed by bourgeois artists, with simply a change of subject-matter. That will result in a reactionary use value. What is required is a 'functional transformation' (Brecht) of 'the forms and instruments of production by a progressive intelligensia . . . in the direction of Socialism'. The epic theatre is, of course, Benjamin's paradigm example, although what is striking is the congruence of this concept with, for instance, Lissitsky's notion of the transformation of art by the political needs of the moment. The argument is developed in a different direction by Benjamin in another influential essay, 'The Work of Art in the Age of Mechanical Reproduction' (in Benjamin, 1970), where the connection between content and technical means of production is explored in relation to film and radio.[16]

Benjamin's work as a whole is complex and convoluted. It includes brilliant unfinished studies of Baudelaire's poetry and its place in 'Paris, capital of the nineteenth century' and essays on various literary themes. In the 1960s, his work was rediscovered by the German 'New Left', and a battle took place between these young Marxist intellectuals and an older generation of Jewish liberals, who claimed that Marxism played a lesser role than Talmudic thought in Benjamin's writing. In his last years, however, Benjamin's intellectual alliances were Marxist, albeit of an unorthodox kind. As well as his relationship with Brecht, Benjamin was in close contact with one of Brecht's most trenchant critics on the left, T. W. Adorno, a leading member of the Frankfurt School.

The group of thinkers associated with the Institute for Social Research at Frankfurt practised a 'critical theory' which was in a symbiotic relationship with Marxism, rather than part of the Marxist mainstream. Besides Adorno, the major figures of the Frankfurt School were Max Horkheimer and Herbert Marcuse, although at various times it had included figures such as Erich Fromm, Leo Lowenthal and the economist Friedrich Pollock. In 1933, the Institute went into exile, to France and then the USA. It was re-established in Frankfurt in 1950 by Adorno and Horkheimer, influencing a younger generation of German philosophers, including Jurgen Habermas and Alfred Schmidt.

From the beginning the Frankfurt School adopted a contemplative attitude towards the politics of the communist movement, and as their work developed in the shadow of Fascist successes, the ambiguity over the question of proletarian revolution became a pessimism as to the possibility of any alternative to the 'authoritarian' stage of capitalism. Such was the view of Marcuse's *One Dimensional Man* (1964), which described the emergence of a managerial capitalism, which had resolved all the contradictions that Marxists had discovered in *laisser faire* capitalism. Ironic-

ally the force of Marcuse's analysis was one of the inspira-
tions behind a new oppositional wave, the 'student revolt'
of the 1960s.

The writings of the Frankfurt School were of two main
kinds: critiques of traditional philosophy and studies of
various cultural or 'superstructural' phenomena. A
common characteristic of the School's culture criticism was
its view of the social system as a totality whose essential
features were to be found at all levels, the cultural as well as
the economic. Nazi Germany, with its total domination of
every aspect of social life offered a manifest example, but
Adorno and Horkheimer also found this 'one dimensional'
structure in capitalist America. They argue that here the
'ticket' system of electoral politics is merely an instance of
the pervasive totalitarianism of the society:

> . . . the basis of the development which leads to ticket thought is
> the universal reduction of all specific energies to a single, equal
> and abstract form of labour, from the battlefield to the film-
> studio. But the transition to a more human situation cannot take
> place, because the same thing happens to the good as the bad.[17]

This bleak view of modern capitalism pervades Adorno's
culture criticism, much of which is concerned with music.
He had studied musicology and also composition with
Alban Berg. His theoretical work, notably the *Philosophy of
Modern Music* (1973) marks the major contribution to a
Marxist theory of music. It is a typical work of the
Frankfurt School in its direct relation of musical structure
to social structure, and in the use of Freudian concepts to
elaborate what Adorno calls 'theory about the listener' in an
essay on popular music.

The *Philosophy of Modern Music* is built around a
dichotomy between two great composers, Schoenberg and
Stravinsky. Schoenberg's atonal music is:

> . . . no longer the mimesis of passions, but rather the undisguised
> registration through the musical medium of bodily impulses from
> the unconscious, of shocks and traumas which assault the taboos
> of form inasmuch as the latter attempt to impose their censorship
> on such impulses, to rationalise them and to transpose them into

images. Thus Schoenberg's formal innovations were innately related to the changes in the things expressed, and helped the new reality of the latter to break through to consciousness. The first atonal works are transcripts, in the sense of the dream transcripts of psychoanalysis.[18]

For Adorno, the musical equivalent of the totally administered society is the system of 'taboos of form', the conventional structures which can on longer express anything except acceptance of what is, the fact of domination. The 'return of the repressed' can only occur through a 'shattering of the social contract with reality' (Adorno, 1974). In contrast to Schoenberg, Stravinsky's music is rooted in the 'social contract with reality'. It expresses a 'pre-individuality' which was strong in nineteenth-century Russia and is resurgent in Soviet Russia. But this calculated primitiveness, the folksiness is for Adorno a demagoguery comparable to that of fascism. The attack on Stravinsky's regressive populism is akin to that on Brecht for his simulation of 'peasant diction'.

Schoenberg emerges from Adorno's analysis as a composer whose work reflects the social totality, but negatively, through negating it. But the negation is only effective as long as the music does not ossify into a system (the twelve-tone system). At that point even Schoenberg is recuperated by the authoritarian social structure. Nevertheless, for Adorno a 'radical music' is possible, one which 'is the antithesis of the industry of culture' and 'attacks false musical consciousness'.

The 'culture industry' includes all light and popular music, as well as the cinema, radio, popular fiction etc. Its function, via certain psychoanalytical mechanisms, is to maintain the mass audience in a state of obedience and submission. In discussing popular music, Adorno is at his strongest when he discusses industrial forms of reproduction and distribution, but on weak ground in describing the musical and psychoanalytical content. Willener (1973) provides a critique of Adorno's assumption that all dance rhythms are structurally equivalent to the authoritarianism of military marching music, and that jazz is essentially sado-masochistic, since it is the blacks' attempt to reproduce white European music through imitation (masochism) or ridicule (sadism).

Adorno's acceptance of the conventional division between 'high' and 'low' art is given a more orthodox Marxist gloss in his correspondence with Benjamin (Adorno/Benjamin, 1967). He criticises the latter's ideas on the revolutionary potential of new cultural forms (cinema, radio) and condemns his position as a capitulation to 'Brechtian motifs', especially:

> . . . the appeal to the immediacy of interconnected aesthetic effects, however fashioned, and to the actual consciousness of actual workers, who have absolutely no advantage over the bourgeois except their interest in the revolution, but otherwise bear all the marks of mutilation of the typical bourgeois.[19]

The hostility of Adorno towards Brecht is based on different arguments to that of Lukacs, although he and the Frankfurt School are often linked together as 'Hegelian' Marxists. For, while Lukacs is suspicious of modernism and its influence on Brecht, for Adorno, Brecht's committed work is not modernist enough. This becomes most clear in the 1950s when both men had returned to different parts of a divided Germany. Brecht's continued adherence to a communism abandoned by Adorno is further proof of the 'bad faith' of his work.

At this stage, Adorno's view was that political reality had become either too complex or serious and horrifying (what art could there be after the concentration camps?) for the simplicity or satire of Brecht's drama to comprehend. He links Brecht's *Arturo Ui* (which presents Hitler as a Chicago gangster) with Chaplin's *The Great Dictator* and says of the latter that it:

> . . . loses all satirical force, and becomes obscene, when a Jewish girl can bash a line of storm-troopers on the head without being torn to pieces. For the sake of political commitment, political reality is trivialised; which then reduces the political effect.[20]

This example dramatises the gulf between the Brechtian concept of art and that held, in different ways, by Adorno and Lukacs. For each of them, 'propaganda' or 'agit-prop' can never be authentic art, since that must in some way reflect or reject the underlying reality of the society. Great art has that cognitive value, the direct insight into reality. For Brecht, however, art is implicated in what a later Marxist generation would call 'ideological struggle', a struggle to 'unmask' the 'prevailing view of things as the view of those who rule'. In that sense it cannot provide direct knowledge of reality in a way comparable to the procedures of science. In order to make a politically effective work of art, the 'distortion' of reality and ridicule are acceptable methods to Brecht (and Chaplin), particularly since Brecht was able to see his own contribution as part of a wider military and political battle.

Ultimately, Adorno's position came to reject all realism, whether that of Brecht or of Lukacs. In the epoch of the totalitarian society, he concluded, 'It is to works of art that has fallen the burden of wordlessly asserting what is barred to politics'. Adorno's bleak view finds no oppositional forces in the contemporary epoch, save those of the most austere *avant-garde* art. His colleague Marcuse, while sharing the same general perspective, found a greater range of artistic work engaged in a critique of the *status quo*, including that of Brecht. He focuses on the Brechtian 'estrangement' or 'alienation effect' (*Verfremdungseffekt*), that confusing term which refers to Brecht's intention that, in his work: 'That which is "natural" must assume the features of the extraordinary. Only in this manner can the laws of cause and effect reveal themselves.'[21] Marcuse links this with a general *avant-garde* project, which is 'literature's own answer to the threat of behaviourism — the attempt to rescue the rationality of the negative'. This project, says Marcuse, links the great radical (Brecht) with the great conservatives of literature (Valéry).

By 1969, in *An Essay On Liberation*, a reconsideration of

the Frankfurt School's pessimism in the light of the 'youth revolt' and the black movement in the USA, Marcuse was able to view certain *avant-garde* developments in the arts in a more positive light:

> . . . these are not merely new modes of perception reorientating and intensifying the old ones; they rather dissolve the very structure of perception, in order to make room — for what? The new object of art is not yet given, but the familiar object has become impossible, false. From illusion, imitation, harmony to reality — but the reality is not yet 'given'.[22]

The work of Marcuse and Adorno represents an ambitious attempt to produce an aesthetic combining Marx, Freud and the twentieth-century *avant-garde* in a rearguard action against the encroachment of a totalitarian economic system and its satellite culture. Against them, Brecht and Lukacs are united in defining the problems of art and literature in terms of a new 'realism'. But in constructing that realism, Lukacs looks for a modern equivalent of the 'great realism' of the past, while Brecht wants an artistic representation of the specific characteristics and contradictions of contemporary societies. In addition to these contrasting versions of 'socialist realism', a third was to emerge in the 1940s, in the context of a very different revolutionary struggle. For just as the political strategy of the Chinese Revolution differed drastically from that of the Russian, although it was described in similar terms, so the Chinese version of socialist realism, while sharing the same name, defined a distinctly separate practice of revolutionary art.

BIBLIOGRAPHICAL NOTE

On Lukacs, see Jameson (1971), Lichtheim (1970) and Zitta (1964). Three critical articles on his work, from varying perspectives, are Sparks (1973), Stedman Jones (1971) and Revai (1971). Gallas (1973) provides an account of the issues at stake in his debate with Brecht.

Brecht's work in English is available in Willett (1964). Useful discussions of his ideas are to be found in Benjamin

(1973), Barthes (1964) and the special number of *Screen* (1974, Vol. 15, no. 2). A Soviet view is to be found in Leizerov (1969). Witt (1975) consists of memoirs by his co-workers. Benjamin has been written about very little in English, but see the introductions to his two books, Brewster (1968) and Jameson (1971).

Jay (1973) gives a full history of the Frankfurt School. Therborn (1970) is a hostile review of its basic ideas. Jameson (1971) has chapters on both Adorno and Marcuse.

Chapter Four

SOCIALIST REALISM IN CHINA

1. LU HSUN AND THE GARRETS OF SHANGHAI

THE official description of literature and art in contemporary China states that it should integrate 'revolutionary realism with revolutionary romanticism . . . to enable literature and art better to serve the workers, peasants and soldiers'.[1] At first sight little seems to differentiate such a formulation from the classical definitions of Soviet socialist realism in the 1930s. Indeed a cursory glance at the texts produced under this imprimatur and published in translation in the journal *Chinese Literature* and various collections of short stories or *Songs to Chairman Mao* might suggest to a Western observer that Chinese artistic production since the Revolution of 1949 follows closely the lines laid down in the 'worst' phase of Stalinism in the Soviet Union: personality cult of Mao, narrowly-defined themes of revolutionary struggle and victory, heroes and heroines of shining virtue and devotion.

To come to this conclusion, however, is to ignore the specific history of Chinese art in its relationship to the revolutionary practice of the last half-century, and to ignore Marx's own comment that one must analyse something from the side of production rather than consumption. For the originality of the Marxist aesthetic developed within the Chinese Revolution lies in its precise re-definition of the relations of production of art-works in China, and the place of such activity within a whole network of ideological/writing practices, dominated by the famous wall-posters, the *tatzupao*.

Writing is in fact a crucial term from which to begin to

69

understand the momentum and trajectory of cultural policy and practice in China. The notion of the written is already inscribed in the Chinese word for culture, *wenhua*. *Wen* means, in the words of the German scholar Schickel, 'the written in the highest sense of the word, the written text. *Hua* means 'to change, to become transformed, to evolve, to become something through what is written, to become a scholar'.[2] In traditional, Imperial China, possession of culture in this sense was a necessary qualification for a position of power, as political official or magistrate. In post-Imperial China, literacy and acquisition of culture of a different kind has also been closely linked to politics.

This is the continuing theme which linked the formative May 4th Movement of 1919, led by progressive intellectuals against the cultural hegemony of the old ruling strata, with the cultural struggle waged by the Communist Party led by Mao Tse Tung, whose key text is the *Talks At The Yenan Forum On Art And Literature* of 1942. In 1927 Lu Hsun, the writer who more than any other straddled the two movements, summed up the issues at stake in the literacy question:

> One of the differences between civilised men and savages is that civilised men have writing to convey their thoughts and feelings to the rest of the world and posterity. China also has writing, but a writing quite divorced from the mass of the people. Couched in crabbed, archaic language, it describes outmoded, archaic sentiments. All its utterances belong to the past and therefore amount to nothing. Hence our people, unable to understand each other, are like a great dish of loose sand.[3]

This statement remains very much within the liberal problematic of the May 4th Movement, which was strongly influenced by contemporary Western democratic, literary and technocratic thought. The dominant mode of writing is condemned because it is incapable of contributing to the 'modernisation' of China, while the people need their own forms of writing in order to rise above savagery and to communicate with each other. At this time, in fact, Lu Hsun

(1881-1936) was moving leftwards and two years later would take part in the founding of the League of Left-Wing Writers in Shanghai. There, the all-important strategic purpose of mass literacy would be added to the liberal programme and transform it into a communist one: 'To combat the ideological tendencies of the petty-bourgeoisie, which has "lost its position in society". We support and work for the emergence of a proletarian art and literature.'[4]

These were the tasks to which Lu Hsun devoted himself in the later years of his life. He had started as a poet and short story writer, whose best known work of fiction was the sardonic *True Story Of Ah Q*. Now he concentrated on the short essay, a form pioneered by the May 4th Movement to concentrate its satiric assault on the ancien regime in culture. In the Preface to his last collection of prose pieces (1935), Lu Hsun wrote of the tactical importance of his chosen form:

> . . . at an urgent time like this, the writer's task is to react or fight back immediately against what is harmful, to serve as sensory nerves, as limbs to resist and attack. It is, of course, very fine to devote oneself to producing a monumental masterpiece for the sake of the civilisation of the future; however, writers fighting for the present are embattled both for the present and the future, for if we lose the present, we have no future either.[5]

The tone of urgency in this passage was in part a product of the intense ideological battles amongst the radicalised intelligentsia of Shanghai during the 1920s and 1930s, within which Lu Hsun attempted to establish a theoretical position distinct from that of those writers who wished to keep literature free from 'contamination' by politics or those who had a crude and undeveloped commitment to revolutionary literature. But, more importantly, the political defeats of the Communist Party in the urban centres of China effectively cut off Lu Hsun and other members of the League of Left Wing Writers from any kind of mass audience. Instead, their work was only available to 'a section of the students, office workers and shop assistants', as Mao was to say later.[6]

This embattled situation clearly influenced Lu Hsun's emphasis in a major essay, *A Glance At Shanghai Literature*, on the difficulty of creating a proletarian literature:

> In a society like China today, the best we can hope for is the appearance of works showing the revolt of the petit-bourgeoisie against their own class, or works of exposure. For a writer who has grown up in a dying class has a deep understanding of and hatred for it, and so he can deal a most powerful mortal blow.[7]

However correct this might have been for Shanghai, in the same year (1929), the Chinese Communist Party officially inaugurated its own policy of proletarian cultural work within the Red Army in the liberated areas of the countryside. It was resolved that art and literary work should be central to the political education of the soldiers, using wall newspapers, songs, drum dances and drama. This marked the start of a major 'agitprop' movement within the Red Army and its revolutionary bases, culminating in the Yenan Forum, over which Mao presided in 1942.

Lu Hsun's contribution was nevertheless an important one for Marxist writing as a whole, and in contemporary China he is honoured as the great precursor of today's cultural policies. For if his writings, for determinate historical reasons, did not qualify as proletarian literature in the direct sense, they did much to specify the necessary conditions for the emergence of such literature. Additionally, many of his best essays were critiques of various aspects of petty-bourgeois and bourgeois ideology — precisely those aspects which Gramsci had defined as 'common sense'. Two representative pieces, on public reactions to a mother's suicide and the hypocritical Western attitude towards animals, are included in Gladys Yang's selection of his work.[8] In an important sense this critique of ideologies of everyday life looks forward to Roland Barthes' *Mythologies*,[9] which performs a similar task within a very different class society.

2. MAO AND THE REVOLUTIONARY BASES

In *Talks At The Yenan Forum On Art and Literature*, Mao pays due homage to the work of Lu Hsun, in the course of a text whose application of the dialectic to pertinent concrete problems matches the skill of the Shanghai writer's best essays. Nevertheless, he emphasises that the problems of proletarian art in Yenan are far removed from those of the cities: 'To come to the revolutionary bases from the garrets of Shanghai (as many of Lu Hsun's co-thinkers and followers did) means not only to pass from one place to another, but from one historical epoch to another.'[10]

Since the Liberation of 1949, this lengthy text has become the central reference point for cultural and artistic policy in China. Generally, the use of quotations from it in a whole series of disputes over the nature of the revolutionary line in art have not been of a mechanical kind, inserted in a text primarily to gain prestige for its theses. As with Mao's writings on philosophy, in the famous *Selected Quotations* (the so-called *Little Red Book*), the Yenan text has proved to have a certain productivity, an ability not to provide ready-made thought, but to provoke thought in its readers. Collections of brief articles have been published in translation which describe the way in which Mao's statements on the nature of contradiction have been applied by workers and peasants to solve specific problems encountered in their labour.[11]

In his Yenan Talks Mao unambiguously announces the importance of art for the revolutionary struggle, in a phrase which continues to define the role of artistic practice in Chinese society. Although subordinate to political struggle, he says, art and literature are necessary 'for uniting our own ranks and defeating the enemy'.[12] The correct form of such art, he says, is socialist realism, which he defines in conventional fashion, in terms derived ultimately from Engels' influential dicta: '. . . life as reflected in works of literature and art can and ought to be on a higher plane,

more intense, more concentrated, more typical, nearer the
ideal and therefore more universal than actual everyday life
. . . Revolutionary art and literature should create a variety
of characters out of everyday life and help the masses to
propel history forward.'[13]

Mao also delineates a model of the production process of
art-works, prescribing in general terms their raw material
and means of production. The raw materials are the life of
the people: '. . . materials that are crude but most vital rich
and fundamental; they make all literature and art seem
pallid by comparison; they provide literature and art with
an inexhaustible source, their only source.'[14] Among the
means of artistic production are the examples of 'the
literature and art of ancient times and foreign countries',
critically assimilated. 'It makes a difference, whether or not
we have such examples, the difference between crudeness
and refinement, roughness and polish, between a high and
low level and between slower and faster work.'[15]

Thus far this is a standard socialist realist model, with
varying emphases. What makes Mao's position decisively
different is what might be called, continuing the metaphor,
the relations of production of revolutionary art. These concern the need to produce for the proletariat rather than any
other class within a popular alliance, which is only possible
for an artist who has struggled to achieve for himself the
class position of the proletariat. Here is the source of one of
the recurrent major themes in Chinese cultural policy: the
need for intellectuals continually to revolutionise themselves, to destroy tendencies which work to perpetuate the
division between mental and manual labour. In the *Talks
At The Yenan Forum* Mao insists at length on the difficulty
of this problem for an individual petty-bourgeois intellectual: 'It requires a long period of time, at least eight or
ten years to solve it thoroughly.'[16]

He draws on his experience to portray vividly the
meaning of this shift in class position and its depth. It is not
simply a question of ideas, but one of *feelings* as well. When

he was a student, he recalls, he regarded workers and peasants as dirty. He would not have considered putting on clothes belonging to a worker, whereas he had no qualms about borrowing clothes from fellow intellectuals. But after he became a revolutionary and went to live among the masses, he came to feel that 'in the last analysis, the workers and peasants were the cleanest people and, even though their hands were soiled and their feet were smeared with cow dung, they were really cleaner than the bourgeois and petty-bourgeois intellectuals'.[17] For the British reader the passage recalls George Orwell's similar observations about class and smells in *The Road To Wigan Pier*, though the conclusions drawn are diametrically different.

As well as establishing these general theses about the production of revolutionary art, Mao deals with more detailed aspects of the proletarian standpoint in art, which had been the subject of debate at the Yenan Forum. Distinctions had been made between works that 'popularise' and those which 'raise the standards' of the masses. Mao argues that both approaches are required and are dialectically connected, though popularisation, producing art comprehensible to the masses using folk traditions and vernacular language, is primary. Here, Mao mediates between two one-sided views of revolutionary art, the leftist agitprop attitude (which he describes elsewhere as the 'poster and slogan style') and that committed primarily to the maintenance of 'artistic standards', where those standards are not defined or scrutinized from a political standpoint. One over-politicises art, while the other separates art from politics.

Mao goes on to examine the relationship between politics and aesthetics in general, in a discussion of the tasks of Marxist criticism. He emphasises that the two are distinct from each other in the production of the work of art, thus implicitly placing himself against those Marxists, e.g. Lukacs in the German debate of the 1930s, who argue that certain techniques implicly carry a progressive or reactionary charge. Of the two, states Mao, politics is dominant: 'Some works which politically are downright reactionary may have a certain artistic quality. The more reactionary their content and the higher their artistic quality, the more poisonous they are to the people and the more necessary it is to reject them.'[17] He concludes by calling for a unity of the political and the aesthetic, content and form, in proletarian art.

This aspect of the *Talks At The Yenan Forum* is clearly not fully theorised, which in itself is an indication of where the main aspects of the asethetic field lie for Mao. He is concerned with clarifying the elements of the mode of production of revolutionary art, ensuring the productivity of revolutionary artists, rather than in regulating or legislating for, the precise forms of the finished products.

Nevertheless, the concrete nature of the discussion is emphasised when Mao concludes the *Talks* by considering a series of 'muddled ideas' which writers commonly have in attempting to produce proletarian art. These range from issues of 'common sense', of the type Lu Hsun covered in his essays (human nature, love) to questions of style and structure: the balance between 'extolling and exposing', the use of satire, the need to eulogise. Finally, Mao takes up the question of the relationship between Marxism and 'creative writing':

> Then does not Marxism destroy the creative mood? Yes, it does. It definitely destroys creative moods that are feudal, bourgeois, petty-bourgeois, liberalistic, individualist, nihilist, art-for-art's-sake, aristocratic, decadent or pessimistic, and every other creative mood that is alien to the masses of the people and to the proletariat. So far as proletarian writers and artists are concerned, should not these kinds of creative moods be destroyed? I think they should; they should be utterly destroyed. And while they are being destroyed, something new can be constructed.[19]

3. CULTURAL STRUGGLE WITHIN SOCIALISM

Although Lenin frequently spoke about the need for the political and economic revolution in Russia to be secured by a cultural revolution, that emphasis hardly survived his death in 1924. In China, however, an insistence on the continuing need for ideological struggle within the revolution has been at the forefront of cultural policy since 1949. On the artistic front, the struggle between the 'two lines' has drawn on the lines of demarcation set up by the *Talks At The Yenan Forum*.

During the early 1950s, a group of writers led by Hu Feng, an old colleague of Lu Hsun, protested at the Party's dominance over literature suggesting that only if a writer was free of such direction could he or she produce work of the quality demanded by the revolution. Hu Feng was defeated and imprisoned in 1955, but the following year, Chou En-lai argued that a distinction should be made between writers who were anti-revolutionary and those who supported the revolution while holding mistaken intellectual outlooks. This inaugurated the policy of 'Let A Hundred Flowers Bloom', which in turn was succeeded by a mobilisation of the arts in support of the Great Leap Forward in 1958.

In a development very similar to the 'literature of fact' and 'shock workers of literature' during the first Soviet Five Year Plan, authors and artists were despatched to the factories and the countryside both to record the struggle for production through their own work and to encourage and collect the art of the masses. This method of struggle against the 'petty-bourgeois' attitudes amongst writers had, it was claimed, replaced the administrative measures of earlier years by the time of the Cultural Revolution itself in 1966.

According to Hao Ran, one of the most popular novelists in China, the Cultural Revolution carried further the kind of reforms necessary to produce the correct relationships of artistic production called for in Mao's Yenan Talks. 'The decrease in the importance of the individual was most visible in the writing and publication fields. To some extent, a writer before the Cultural Revolution carried over some of the old idea of writing to establish oneself as a writer, but after 1970 the writer, the publisher and the reader became one, working together to make literature better serve the revolution.'[19]

Hao Ran's own method of work provides an example of this new literary process. After completion of a novel in 1971, he circulated it among first his professional colleagues, and then two hundred communes and factories, to get detailed responses and criticisms. These were considered and, often incorporated into the final text. In addition, every professional writer has been required to assist 'worker-writers' to improve their work, through regular workshops held in the community, or through detailed work on manuscripts considered suitable for publication. The 'shop-floor' writers themselves are allowed paid leave in order to work with a professional like Hao Ran to improve and prepare their work for publication.

These new, proletarian authors represent a fourth generation of revolutionary writers in China. The first two were part of successive generations of radicalised intelligentsia during the 1920s and 1930s. They were those who bore the brunt of Mao's criticisms at Yenan and few of them survived as practising writers into the 1970s. A third generation, typified by Hao Ran, grew up in the years of the revolutionary war, during the 1940s. He has been an agit-prop actor, local and national journalist, and finally author and manuscript editor and collaborator. The cultural policies of the immediate post-Cultural Revolution era implied that a serious attempt was being made, through the 'worker-writers' of the fourth generation to break down the division between mental and manual labour, in which the 'petty bourgeois' mentality of the professional artist was rooted. The defeat of the leftist line in the power struggle following Mao's death may well mean that a policy of encouraging specialisation will spread to the arts as well as technology, providing a setback for the 'decrease of the importance of the individual' in the artistic field.

The changes in artistic practice brought about by the Cultural Revolution were most dramatically apparent in the reform of opera and drama instigated by Chiang Ching, Mao's wife and one of the leftist leaders. Until the early 1960s, theatre in China had meant traditional folk theatre, whose themes of 'emperors and generals, useless scholars and sickly maidens' were condemned by Chiang as reactionary and irrelevant to contemporary life. They were replaced by dramatic productions on contemporary themes, which retained traditional techniques of singing and dancing. Such works as *Taking Tiger Mountain By Strategy* and *Red Detachment Of Women* became 'model operas', reproduced and translated by theatre and dance groups all over China.

Since the political defeat of Chiang Ching, one of the 'Gang of Four', these works have come under attack for the narrowness of their 'revolutionary romanticism'. The principal object of such criticism has been the emphasis in Cultural Revolution works on the 'positive hero', to the exclusion of other characteristics. This emphasis was embodied in the influential 'rule of the three contrasts':

> Give prominence to positive characters among all the characters, to heroes among the positive characters, to the principal hero among the heroes. Create special environment, character and personality and use all kinds of artistic media to make the proletarian heroes stand out. Reveal the heroes' inherent communist spirit.[20]

Such a position, it is argued, involves an imbalance between the realism and romanticism of the classic definition of socialist realism. Thus the realism of character development and of the making of history by the masses is excluded in favour of 'creating characters in which the best and highest of the working class is portrayed, unrestricted by real life and people.'[21] These criticisms are similar to some of the attacks on Zhdanov's socialist realism in the Soviet Union during the period following Stalin's death.

Unlike Zhdanov, Mao did not specify in any detail

precisely what the content of revolutionary art should be. His Yenan Talks concentrated instead on the question of the relations of production of art in a socialist society. It remains to be seen what cultural policies flow from the new line in Chinese politics, and how far they measure up to the Yenan dicta.

BIBLIOGRAPHICAL NOTE

Kai-Yu Hsu (1975) provides an account of literary practice in China today. General texts with briefer descriptions of the arts include Macciocchi (1972) and Welbourne (1975). Fei-Ling (1973) is an excellent introduction to the historical background. Examples of current Chinese writing and painting can be found in the monthly *Chinese Literature*.

Weiss (1971) is an illuminating account of Vietnamese revolutionary culture.

Chapter Five

POST-WAR DEVELOPMENTS

1. WRITING AND COMMITMENT

FOR the first decade after 1945, Marxist aesthetics was dominated by the monolithic orthodoxy of Zhdanov's version of socialist realism, whose denunciatory tone was sharpened by the general atmosphere of the Cold War. In the new socialist countries of Eastern Europe, the cultural apparatus echoed the Soviet position. Even Lukacs was not immune from criticism as the politics of the Popular Front gave way to an uncompromising anti-capitalism. On the philosophical front, he had led the onslaught against existentialism with his *Existentialism Or Marxism?* (1948), but in literary matters he was attacked by his fellow-Hungarian Revai because in 'the struggle against fascism, Comrade Lukacs has forgotten the struggle against capitalism — not only during the past five years, but already much earlier. In his fight against imperialist decadence he attempted to confront fascism with the ancient plebeian popular-revolutionary forms and traditions of bourgeois democracy, generalizing, idealizing and mythologizing them . . .'[1] Revai points to the fact that Lukacs had shown little enthusiasm for the products of socialist realism, since his literary models were located in the pre-1848 era which was 'pre-capitalist' but also 'pre-proletarian'.

Apart from the revisionists of socialist realism (Fischer and Garaudy), recent developments in Marxist aesthetics have taken place outside the tradition of socialist realism, which even in the post-Stalin period of the 'thaw' maintained a hostility to the 'modernism' which constituted the main growing points of literature and the arts in non-communist Europe. Consequently, the main contributions to the Marxist theory of art have involved a rapprochement between revolutionary politics and modernism on the one hand, and between Marxist theory and innovations in the 'human sciences' — notably linguistics and psychoanalysis — on the other. The Marxist theory employed has itself been imbued with various 'unorthodox' elements, repressed by official Soviet Marxism: the Russian formalists, Walter Benjamin, the early Lukacs, new readings of Gramsci and of Brecht.

The first elaboration of a political aesthetic outside the ambit of Soviet orthodoxy was that of Jean-Paul Sartre (b. 1905). Although the existentialist philosophy associated with him and with Maurice Merleau-Ponty had been denounced by the communists, the existentialists had aligned themselves with the political left. The apparent apolitical implications of *Being and Nothingness* had, by 1948, been transformed into a statement of political commitment (*engagement*), in his *What is Literature?*, under the impact of Sartre's experience of the anti-Nazi Resistance Movement.

There had been a long history in French culture of 'Fellow-travelling' artists, as well as consciously communist ones. Gide and Rolland had in the pre-war period announced their admiration for the USSR without modifying their 'bourgeois' writing. Malraux, Aragon and Eluard, in contrast, strove to become communist authors. Sartre's position was distinct from both the fellow-travellers and the Party members. Like the surrealists of the 1920s, but in very different terms, he proclaimed a necessary solidarity between a mode of writing and revolutionary commitment, without the latter (through the Party) determining the nature of the former.

He argued therefore that if a writer was to fulfil his duty *as a writer*, he must necessarily become committed:

> If literature is not everything, it is worth nothing. This is what I mean by 'commitment'. It wilts if it is reduced to innocence, or to

songs. If a written sentence does not reverberate at every level of man and society, then it makes no sense. What is the literature of an epoch but the epoch appropriated by its literature?[2]

At the same time Sartre steadfastly opposed the prescriptions of socialist realism. During the period of the 'thaw', he attended the conferences of European writers at Leningrad and Prague, allying himself with the 'revisionists' on such issues as the 'decadence' of modernism. Among other things, he stated, it was 'Freud, Kafka and Joyce . . . who led me to Marxism'.[3]

Sartre's own Marxism is given theoretical form in the *Critique of Dialectical Reason* (1976), whose implications for literary theory are suggested in the introductory volume: 'Valéry is a petit-bourgeois intellectual, no doubt about it. But not every petit-bourgeois intellectual is Valéry. The heuristic inadequacy of contemporary Marxism is contained in those two sentences.'[4] The integration of existentialism's concern for the choices made by the individual writer into the Marxist class analysis will, according to Sartre, provide the necessary *mediations* to show the relation between the writer and his class position. In his studies of Jean Genet and of Flaubert, Sartre has tried to construct this complex of mediations. In the Flaubert study, they are primarily those of the family. There, 'the religion of art of the later Flaubert proves to have been a synthesis between the religious devotion of a mother of aristocratic origins and the analytical scepticism of a middle-class father only a generation away from the soil'. The contradictions set up in this context are transposed into the novels as 'moments of a total movement which is the very process of inventing a solution to the problems of class conflict faced by Flaubert as a child in the family situation, under the guise of problems of a psychological order.'[5]

2. GOLDMANN'S GENETIC STRUCTURALISM

Sartre's biographical method thus involves a complex relationship between family structure and class structure, with the author's own position within both family and class determining his relation to each and their relation to each other. A different answer to the problem of author and class was proposed by Lucien Goldmann (1913-1970). Born in Bucharest, Goldmann did his major work in Paris and in Brussels. His 'genetic structuralist' theory proposed an homology between the form of a literary work and either the 'world view' of a dominant group in pre-capitalist society (in his early work) or the economic structure of a capitalist society.

'World views' were defined by Goldmann as 'ensembles of mental categories which tended towards coherent structures and which were proper to certain privileged social groups, whose thought, feeling and behaviour were orientated towards an overall organisation of interhuman relations and of relations between men and nature.' The importance of atristic creation is that it is in great works of art and philosophy that the 'mental categories' of the social group are most fully realised, not through the reflection of that group's social life, but through 'creating on the imaginary plane a universe whose content may differ entirely from that of collective consciousness, but whose structure is akin, or even homologous.'[6]

This is the theory which underlies Goldmann's first major work, *The Hidden God*, in which he shows the tragic vision inherent in the works of Pascal and Racine to be homologous with the situation of the *noblesse de la robe* in seventeenth century French society. The origins of the theory lie in the early works of Lukacs, *The Theory Of The Novel* and *History and Class Consciousness*. From the latter Goldmann takes the notion of 'collective consciousness' as world view. Lukacs had posited a gap between the *actual* and *potential* consciousness of a class, the latter representing its full self-knowledge, its understanding of its place in the social structure. Transposing these ideas from politics to culture, Goldmann finds the literary work of the great author approximating most closely to that 'potential consciousness'. A lesser author could reflect only 'actual consciousness'.

From *The Theory Of The Novel* came Goldmann's concept of literary *form* as central to a work's meaning. This notion of form, however, differed from Lukacs' development of the concept in his mature work, where it came to be synonomous with a particular epistemology of realism, the organic unification of essence and appearance. In Goldmann's *For a Sociology of the Novel*, form refers variously to plot structure or literary style (e.g. the *nouveau roman*). Thus, the characteristic novel of the emergent capitalist era takes the form of a 'degraded search' by a 'problematic hero' for authentic values.

This literary form is not, however, homologous with the consciousness of a particular social group. Instead it structurally reproduces the nature of 'everyday life in the individualistic society created by market production. There is a *rigorous homology* between the literary form of the novel . . . and the everyday relation between man and commodities in general, and by extension between men and other men in a market society.' The hero is problematic since he cannot embody any authentic values, which are only present in the novel by implication. This, according to Goldmann, is precisely homologous with the role of the use-value of a commodity in a capitalist society dominated by exchange-value. Its 'action assumes an implicit character, exactly like that of authentic values in the fictional world'.[7] *Stop*

For Goldmann, this is only one phase of the relationship between the novel and capitalist society. In a second phase, corresponding to the development of 'an economy of monopolies and trusts' there is 'the novel of the dissolution of character' (Kafka, Joyce, Camus), which is paralleled philosophically by existentialism. Finally, since the Second World War, there is 'the capitalism of organisation and a consumer society, and the appearance of a new novel and a theatre centred on absence and the impossibility of communication . . .'.[8] This is related to a philosophy of ahistorical structuralism. As a coda to this periodisation of culture, Goldmann's late work on the plays of Genet find in them a new theme of revolt, in a society within which the opositional forces had seemed to be growing weaker.

How is it that in bourgeois society the literary work is no longer the product of a collective consciousness, but relates directly to the substructure of the society? Goldmann's answer appears to be a variant on the traditional Marxist view that capitalism is in principle inimical to art, a statement made by Marx, but never fully elaborated. In Goldmann's account the nature of the capitalist system of exchange and a certain 'false consciousness' on the part of the bourgeoisie both contribute to the 'gap' between social group and works of art.

The crucial point seems to be that the 'authentic values' sought by the problematic hero in Goldmann's archetypal classic novel are precisely those values repressed by capitalism itself. This novel form is therefore 'bound up certainly with history and the development of the bourgeoisie, but not the expression of the real or possible consciousness of that class'.[8] Goldmann goes on to speculate that a further reason for the bourgeoisie not developing any alternative cultural expression is because 'valid literary and cultural creation' can only occur when

> man conceives himself or feels himself as part of a developing whole and situates himself in a historical or transcendent trans-individual dimension. But bourgeois ideology, bound up like bourgeois society itself with the existence of economic activity, is precisely the first ideology in history that is both radically profane and ahistorical . . . [it] created the first radically nonaesthetic form of consciousness (rationalism).[9]

One further reason might be advanced for the non-class nature of the novel in Goldmann's theory: the fact that it is homologous not with economic *production*, in which classes are clearly and antagonistically delineated, but with the process of *exchange*, in which all are 'consumers' of commodities. In fact, the third phase of capitalism, in Goldmann's view, was marked by the collapse of the work of art to the level of 'passive consumption, entertainment and leisure'. His political perspectives, too, involved the opinion that there was no longer any class struggle within production of the kind Marx regarded as constitutive of capitalism, although the events of 1968 caused him to conclude that there was still a rebellion against 'reification', a homology perhaps with the plays of Genet.

Goldman's genetic structuralism has been criticised for the rigidity of the homologies it contains. Glucksmann (1969) points to three kinds of mediation between literary work and social class which Goldmann ignores or rejects. First, there is Sartre's biographical mediation, in which the work is the expression of an individual writer, himself formed in the matrix of family and class; secondly, the formalist emphasis on the 'relative autonomy' of literary tradition, which affects the author's choice of style or theme; and finally, the author's conscious literary ideology, which is particularly crucial for modernist writers whose reflections on their work have the rigour of theory.

Glucksmann takes the last two modes of mediation to produce a critique of Goldmann's reading of the works of Robbe-Grillet, whose novels represent the literary expression of the intense reification of human relationships in the consumerist phase of modern capitalism. In his books, Goldmann concludes, things are more real than people, and the true character of modern society is exposed. However, Glucksmann is able to show that Robbe-Grillet's stated intention is to combat the anthropomorphism of the traditional novel, where a sentimental humanism has endowed objects with human qualities. That, for a humanist Marxist, was a positive act in traditional fiction, since it 'humanised the world'. But from the viewpoint of an opposing school of Marxism, Robbe-Grillet's materialism might be said to posit a link between reification (turning people into things) and anthropomorphism (turning things into people). The two processes could then be said to constitute the opposite sides of the same coin, since they collapse the distinction between man and nature.

Finally, Goldmann's theory shares certain limitations with that of Lukacs. The privileged character of the novel in its ability to reflect social reality is never argued for, so that the role of poetry, painting, music or the cinema in relation to it remains problematic. Beyond that, the rejection of the possibility that the bourgeoisie can give rise to an art-form is generalised to bourgeois society as a whole. It would seem that there is no room in Goldmann's theoretical schema for a culture of the working-class within capitalism, perhaps because his political conclusions point to the integration of that class into the system.

3. ALTHUSSER AND GRAMSCI: THE IMPORTANCE OF IDEOLOGY

Goldmann termed his method 'genetic structuralism" to acknowledge his debt to the psychologist Jean Piaget, but also to distinguish it from that 'ahistorical structuralism' which he saw as no more than the last of the bourgeois ideologies. The wide range of theory and practice encompassed by the term has been a dominant force in the development of the human sciences in general over the last twenty years, and elements of it have been incorporated into the most influential schools of Marxist cultural criticism to emerge in France. In those schools an orientation derived originally from the structural linguistics of Saussure has combined with certain concepts of psychoanalysis to produce a 'semiotic' approach to the ideological level of the superstructure, a concept which itself is now in question.

This complex body of work, which has addressed itself to certain key lacunae in Marxist theory, can best be approached through the work of three seminal figures: the Italian theorist Antonio Gramsci, the Marxist philosopher Louis Althusser and the doyen of semiology,

Roland Barthes. Althusser situated his work as a *return* to the concerns of classical Marxism-Leninism, to develop and re-affirm it in the face of the various 'neo-Hegelian' and 'humanist' interpreters of Marx, amongst whom he included both Goldmann and Sartre. He did this in the context of the structuralist developments in French intellectual life, borrowing and re-casting concepts from other disciplines. Althusser himself strenuously denied any kinship between his work and that of the 'structuralists', although some of his followers suggested this in their own writings (Godelier, 1970).

The correctness of Althusser's ideas have been the subject of much controversy, and his direct influence has undoubtedly waned in the period since the appearance of his first book, *For Marx* (1969, French edition 1965). Yet his intervention, to use one of his own terms, has undoubtedly lifted the level of Marxist theoretical discussion in Western Europe, thanks to his insistence on the rigorous exposition of concepts and ideas.

Pierre Macherey's *Pour une théorie de la production littéraire* (1966) is the one major attempt to apply Althusser's ideas specifically to literature, while Terry Eagleton's *Literature and Ideology* (1976) is influenced by Macherey's approach. Macherey's title refers to one of Althusser's most important innovations, the translation of Marx's concept of production from the economic sphere to the other levels of the social formation. Thus a theoretical, ideological or aesthetic product is also the result of the application of means of labour to transform a raw material. Macherey's book examines not the finished product in isolation, but as the result of the process of literary production. In doing so he re-reads Lenin's articles on Tolstoy as the 'Mirror of the Revolution', in the 'symptomatic' manner applied by Althusser to Marx.

The 'symptomatic reading' is a concept of psychoanalysis, where it describes 'the Freudian analyst's reading of his patient's utterances'.[10] The Althusserian variant concerns the construction of the 'problematic' or underlying structure of concepts (a theory or an ideology) which inform the work, often by their absence as well as their presence. The result, in Macherey's work, is 'the total abandonment of a unified notion of the literary work as a finished form capable of resolving the conflicts of reality to which it is a response'.

In contrast to the Lukacsian idea of great art, which has direct access to reality through its 'reflection' of it, for Macherey, artistic production takes place entirely within ideology, although art itself is not simply ideological. The concept of ideology involved, and the place within it of the 'structuralist' psychoanalytical theory of Jacques Lacan, represent Althusser's major contribution to the new Marxist aesthetics. Lacan's concept of the human 'subject' provides a theory of ideology with a way of escaping from the notion of ideological *manipulation* of the masses by the rulers, which previous theories had implied (e.g. the Frankfurt School on the culture industry). For Lacan, the subject is

> de-centred, constituted by a structure that has no 'centre' either, except in the imaginary misrecognition of the 'ego', i.e. in the ideological formations in which it 'recognises' itself.[11]

Ideology, here, refers not to a system of 'wrong ideas' (as opposed to the truth of science), but to the whole terrain of conscious — and unconscious — experience. In Althusser's terms, it is 'the "lived" relation between men and their world, or a reflected form of this unconscious relation, for instance a "philosophy" '.[12] The characteristic form of ideology in general is spontaneous *recognition*.

The relevance of all this for a theory of art becomes clear in Althusser's three occasional pieces on artistic matters.[13] In the 'Letter to Daspre', he denies art a parallel status with science, but argues that great art is not simply ideological:

> What art makes us *see*, and therefore gives to us in the form of 'seeing', 'perceiving', 'feeling', is the ideology from which it is born, in which it bathes, from which it detaches itself as art, and to which it alludes.[14]

In relation to Brecht, Althusser adds elsewhere: 'His principal aim is to produce a critique of the spontaneous ideology in which men live.'[15] Brecht achieves this by replacing the central focus on the 'full ego' of the hero (and producing an irrational empathy in the audience) with his 'asymmetrical, decentred' plays. The political importance of this 'decentring' lies in its critique of the notion of the sovereign individual, and its exposure of that individual as structured, or unstructured by social forces. In Brecht's *Good Woman Of Szechuan*, the heroine is split into two characters by the pressure of contradiction in a bourgeois society.

A second stage of Althusser's theory of ideology comes with his essay 'Ideology and Ideological State Apparatuses' (Althusser, 1971). This is an attempt to place the theory of ideology in general into a Marxist schema of the social formation, in which specific ideologies have their effect. He grapples with the inadequacy of the traditional base/super-structure model and suggests that the active function of ideologies is better explained as the reproduction of the relations of production of the society: the reproduction of the ensemble of habits, moralities, opinions which ensure that the work-force (and those responsible for re-producing them in the family, school etc.) are maintained in their position of subordination to the dominant class.

This reproduction occurs in determinate ways in the range of 'Ideological State Apparatuses'', which include the family, church, legal system, education system, trade unions, political institutions, and the cultural and communications media. These are the loci of the reproduction of ideologies, but also of ideological struggles, between the ideologies of different classes. In the current situation, Althusser suggests, the educational Ideological State Apparatus is the strategic one. To test this hypothesis, Renée Balibar and others undertook a study of the function of literature and language within the education system.[16] This represents a shift, as Macherey has emphasised, from the 'formalism' of his earlier book, which represents the realisation that 'You cannot study the production of literature without studying its reproduction'.[17] The ideological significance of a text is therefore determined by the relation between the book and the context in which it is actualised (the ideological structures of the institution — 'school', 'leisure' — in which it is read).

In his later essay on ideology, Althusser acknowledges the pioneering importance in this area of Marxist theory of Antonio Gramsci (1891-1937). A leader of the Italian Communist Party, Gramsci spent the last decade of his life in a Fascist prison, where he composed his *Prison Notebooks* (Gramsci, 1971). Among these fragmentary writings are numerous reflections on the character and place of what later Marxists were to call 'ideological struggle', in a capitalist society which continues to function primarily through the consent of the masses, with armed force to be used only when that consent crumbles. Gramsci addressed himself to the problem of how to disintegrate that structure of consent.

Earlier, in 1919, he had been a founder of the journal *Ordine Nuovo* which united cultural and political material for its readership of the working class of Turin. At first the paper associated itself with the Proletcult movement in the Soviet Union, setting up a local Institute of Proletarian Culture in 1921. In order to produce its own art and culture, Gramsci argued at this point, the proletariat must engage in the general problems of history, art, literature, morality, education and technology.[18] He wrote drama criticism for *Ordine Nuovo* and supplied Trotsky with information on Italian Futurism for his *Literature and Revolution*.

By the 1930s the insurrectionary fervour of the Turin years had been supplanted by the concept of a 'war of position' during which the Marxist party would need to struggle to establish a proletarian 'hegemony' of culture and consciousness over the ruling class.[19] In discussing this struggle, Gramsci emphasised three things: its universal character, its presence in philosophical theory and the 'common sense' ideas of everyday life alike; the contradictory nature of much popular thought and belief, so that elements of 'common sense' ideologies could be detached and re-placed in a hegemonic ideology; and the importance of intellectuals in this struggle.[20]

For Gramsci, intellectuals were of two kinds, the organic and the traditional. Organic intellectuals were peculiar to a particular rising or ruling class, performing functions essential to that class's assumption or maintenance of power. Traditional intellectuals were the functionaries of 'pre-existing' institutions common to all class societies: education, the law, the arts. The organic intellectuals of the working-class were thus, in Gramsci's view, a strategic factor in the ideological struggle:

> The mode of existence of the new intellectual can no longer consist of eloquence, the external and momentary arousing of sentiments and passions, but must consist of being actively involved in practical life, as a builder, an organiser, 'permanently persuasive' because he is not purely an orator . . .[21]

This new intellectual is a 'specialist plus politician', a definition which recalls the mixture of technique and politics in the definitions of socialist art by Mayakovsky and Benjamin.

Michel Foucault has more recently developed a conception of the political situation of intellectuals which contains echoes of Gramsci's theory. (Foucault, 1977.) In it, he contrasts the traditional left-wing intellectual who was 'the master of truth and justice . . . the representative of the universal' with the new 'specific' intellectuals. The latter work not in 'The just-and-true-for-all', but in specific sectors, at precise points where they are situated either by their professional conditions of work or their conditions of life. Unlike Gramsci's 'specialist plus politician', this specific intellectual is determined by his place in the social formation, although in other respects the two are similar in their characteristics. Foucault's definition of the traditional intellectual, with its implicit critique, is perhaps especially applicable to the artistic field. For what is a great novelist for Lukacs but a 'master of truth and justice'?

4. BARTHES, MYTH AND THE SIGNIFIER

Foucault is himself one of that series of authors and theorists whose various 'structuralisms' have acted as a stimulus to Marxist thought in all areas in the last two decades. Unlike most, however, his work consists not of a general theory, but of a number of investigations into particular areas of social practice, each of which is united by a controlling 'discourse' whose structures determine the procedures and limits of medicine, natural history or the analysis of wealth. The order and security of the discourse is maintained by a pattern of exclusion, of those whose language or behaviour violates its rules. In this way the 'mad' are defined in *Madness and Civilisation*, while the notion of exclusion is taken up by Philippe Sollers in his *Logiques*, where it is applied to literature. Writers whose work is 'unreadable' because of subject-matter (Sade) or mode of writing (Mallarmé, Joyce) are shown to have broken the taboos of the dominant discourse of literature.

In *The Order Of Things* (1970), Foucault argued that the discourses of a particular historical period were rooted in an *épistémè*, 'the tacit experience of order as such, which stands between the fundamental codes of a culture (those which govern its language, its perceptions, its modes of exchange, its techniques, its values and practices) and the scientific and philosophical interpretations it produces'.[22] If there can be said to be any common perspective amongst the variety of 'structuralists', from Lacan to Lévi-Strauss, Foucault to Althusser, it lies in their resistance to what Foucault names as the essential feature of the contemporary *épistémè*, the placing of Man as the origin of social practice.

The disintegration of this *épistémè* was begun by Marx and Freud, one from the 'outside', showing that social being determines consciousness, the other from the inside with the demonstration of the power of the unconscious. The modern structuralist theory of the aesthetic begins with Roland Barthes' *Writing Degree Zero* (Barthes, 1967) first published in 1953. One of the three elements involved in literature, a language is:

> a horizon, and style a vertical dimension, which together map out for the writer a Nature, since he does not choose either . . . In the former, he finds a familiar History, in the latter a familiar personal past.[23]

The writer's only moment of choice concerns his 'mode of writing'. Within the strict, historical, limits of the possible, this represents 'the writer's consideration of the social use which he has chosen for his form, and his commitment to this choice'. According to Barthes this 'choice' became axiomatic in French literature after the 1848 Revolution, when the transparent, unproblematic, classical mode of writing (bourgeois writing) 'became merely one among many possible others' as the bourgeoisie imposed itself as a ruling class, no longer able to present itself as the repository of universal values. (In important respects, this analysis matches Lukacs' view of the turning-point of 1848. But because the classical mode equals great art for Lukacs, he has to seek its re-appearance elsewhere. He finds it with Tolstoy in Russia, a country which had not had its 1848 revolution.)

While parts of *Writing Degree Zero* are marked by a Sartrean emphasis, the concept of a mode of writing — not 'content' or 'tendency' — as the link between writer and society, points forward to Barthes' next book, *Mythologies* (first published in 1957), which has been described as a *'semiologie engagée'*. Semiology was the science of signs and signifying systems proposed by the structural linguist Ferdinand de Saussure, of which linguistics itself would form only a part. Saussure's influential work became the model for much later 'structuralist' writing because of the way he described language as a 'system of relations' rather than a collection of words or a series of utterances. He re-thought both the nature of the linguistic sign and the system of language itself. Each was constituted in Saussure's theory by the interdependence of two elements. The sign was composed of signifier and signified, the language involved a system of rules (*langue*) and its enact-ment (*parole* or speech). Within the sign, the signifier was the sound-image and the signified the concept or mental representation. The relationship between the two in language was characteristically an arbitrary one: the sounds or written symbols which were the form of the signifier had a relationship with the signified fixed by convention, through a system of difference (e.g. the written alphabet or the range of phonemes in spoken language).

In *Mythologies*, Barthes attempted to politicise this semiotic concept of the sign. The book examines a hetero-geneous collection of aspects of French life — advertise-ments, food, sport, public figures (Billy Graham, Poujade) — to discover the connotations hidden beneath the 'innocence' of their denotations. In order to reveal these connotations, Barthes constructs a two-level sign system. The first sign (whose signifier is two men in a ring, and whose signified is a wrestling match) itself becomes a signifier of a second sign. The signified of this second sign is a certain 'eye for an eye' conception of justice. This process, by which an ideological meaning attaches itself, apparently 'naturally', to an everyday event or object, Barthes calls 'mythification'. Myth itself is then a language system or *langue* (for Saussure, the structure of rules which makes speech possible) and these instances are its speech.

The mythification process, Barthes explains, is the means by which the dominant ideology works to present historic-ally and culturally determined meanings as 'natural'. This naturalisation of the sign operates through a denial or repression of the activity of the signifier, which becomes a transparent (invisible) window onto the 'real' (the signified). The implication is that the 'meaning' of the wrestling match is not innate, but determined by the dominant ideology present in all cultural practices.

This early version of Barthes' semiology is also brought to bear on the question of the novelty of Brechtian theatre. Like Althusser, Barthes sees it as a 'critique of the spontaneous ideology in which men live'. This 'spontaneous ideology' (Barthes' 'myth') is inherent in the conventions of orthodox theatre with its ' "natural" expression of reality'. The method adopted by Brecht however, operates 'a certain distance between the signified and the signifier'.[24] The actor (signifier) is thus no longer *identical* with the character (signified). Instead of identifying with the character, the actor *signifies* it.

After *Mythologies*, Barthes' semiotic investigations were less directly political. He developed the techniques of analysis in *Système De La Mode*, a highly systematic examination of the semiology of Fashion. Elsewhere, he proposed a science of literature to study the process of production of meaning, rather than the various meanings which criticism 'discovered' in literature. This science would then be able to show how a variety of interpretations of the same text were possible.

S/Z (1975), an analysis of Balzac's short story, *Sarrasine*, represented Barthes' most sustained attempt to practice his science of literature. He demonstrated the structuration of the text by the interweaving of five codes throughout the 500 lexies (units of reading) into which he divided the text. The story itself was chosen because of its status as a 'limit-text', a story apparently well within the confines of the classic realist (bourgeois) mode of writing, but in fact lacking

> the plenitude of an ultimate *signifié* (signified), which leaves a network of *signifiants* (signifiers) that circulate without point of rest, in a ceaseless process of making and re-making meaning, a circulation that Balzac in the moment of writing the premisses of the readability of the classic text cannot but feel as trouble . . .[25]

The 'lack' of the ultimate signified is connected by Barthes to the centrality of the theme of castration in Balzac's story, but the principal conclusion of *S/Z* is that the classic, realist, representational novel is also a kind of myth, a presentation of an ideological construct as a mirror of the real, through a similar repression of the signifier. Barthes was an early champion of the *nouveau roman* in France, seeing in it the liberation of the signifier, the recognition of the activity of language. The political implications of his later work for a combative Marxist aesthetic have been explored by a group also originating with the *nouveau roman*, the contributors to the review *Tel Quel*.

5. TEL QUEL AND THE 'UNREADABLE'

Society places two alternative taboos on *écriture* accordingly as it bodies forth works of fiction which transform or challenge a hitherto acceptable formal system, or as it stems from a theoretical practice whose function is to conceptualise both the language-system, i.e. the informational relay which enables society to formulate and exercise its identity, and any new formal system which may arise . . . Its defence mechanisms are therefore directed against those activities which aim to reveal the process of production of objects, whether in the field of industrial production or that of the production of 'meaning'; they are directed against those engaged in critical and theoretical work and especially against those whose work lies along the two axes of *ecriture*: its concrete practice — fiction — and the theoretical formulation of that practice. (Baudry, 1974)

This statement, first published in 1967 is a representative summary of the aesthetic politics of *Tel Quel* at that point. *Ecriture* refers to that practice of writing, exemplified in certain authors of the *nouveau roman*, which challenges the dominance of representational realism. The 'theoretical formulation' of that activity, in the work of the *Tel Quel* group, combined elements of Barthes 'science of literature' with Althusser's generalisation of the Marxist concept of production from economics to all social practices. Just as Marx had analysed not simply the products of capitalism

but their very process of production, so *Tel Quel* set itself
the task of revealing the means by which 'meaning' was
produced by bourgeois society. The strategic importance of
this task lay in the centrality of this process of production
of meaning for capitalism's sense of its own 'identity'.

According to Philippe Sollers, the group's principal
spokesman, fiction itself occupied a crucial place within
that language-system:

> THE NOVEL IS THE WAY IN WHICH THIS SOCIETY
> SPEAKS TO ITSELF, the way in which the individual must live
> to be accepted there. Who are you if not a character from a novel?
> The novel, with the mute quality of science, is the *value* of our
> epoch, in other words its code of instinctive reference, the
> exercise of its power, the key to its everyday unconscious,
> mechanical, shut.[26]

Like Lukacs, Sollers places the novel at the centre of his
theory, although the value assigned to it is totally different.
In so far as the novelistic mode of plot, narrative and
character is distributed throughout many cultural forms —
cinema, television drama, even documentary programmes[27] — this *Tel Quel* position offers a general
critique of the forms of the dominant ideology in capitalist
society.

There are similarities between this position and other
marxist or quasi-marxist standpoints, notably those of
Barthes and of Brecht, whose critique of dominant artistic
modes focussed on their repression of the contradiction
with which bourgeois society and its members are honey-
combed. However, Brecht (not entirely for tactical reasons)
considered himself to be a socialist realist artist, albeit a
'Brechtian' one. But the *Tel Quel* position, as it has
developed, rejects not only 'classic realism' but denies that
representational writing in general can possess revolutionary significance. To this extent, it has moved beyond
established traditions of marxist aesthetics, including the
critical positions of Mayakovsky, Brecht and the
Althusserian school.

The *Tel Quel* group have, nevertheless, remained committed to a revolutionary political position, retained Marx's concept of mode of production within their theory and have made an ambitious attempt to resolve the long-standing problem of the compatibility of the theories of Marx and Freud. This last area has dominated the most recent work of the review and of its key theoretical figure, Julia Kristeva. Much of the impetus for that work came from the existence of two lacunae in the earlier *Tel Quel* theory. The first concerned the new definition of semiotics as the study of the process of production of signs, rather than their meanings. The difficulty lay in actually theorising this production and the space in which it occurred: 'that other scene of the before-sense production of sense' (Kristeva). The 'other scene' could only be conceptualised through psychoanalytic theory, notably that of Jacques Lacan, the French theoretician, whose re-interpretation of Freud had been made with concepts borrowed from structural linguistics. The second gap in the theory also found its solution in Lacan's ideas. *Tel Quel* had previously followed the Formalists in rejecting the notions of omnipotent Author and passive Reader. Nevertheless, writing and reading were practices with practitioners: Lacan's notion of the human 'subject' offered a radically anti-humanist account of the human individual implicated in signifying practices.

In Kristeva's theory, the subject is one of the most important concepts taken over from Lacan. Unlike the free or self-determining unified individual of humanist thought, the subject is complex, ever-changing and the site of contradictions produced by the action of social institutions and signifying practices. Thus, within the subject there is a certain antagonistic relationship between forces defined by Kristeva as those of 'unity' and 'process':

> The regulations of the relations of production by the state and the legal system, together with the regulation of reproduction by the family, hold in place a certain type of relation between *unity* and *process* in the economy of the speaking subject, at the same time as

being themselves consolidated by this relation. The form of the relation consists in the privileging of the unifying instance (the instance which established the coherence of the sign, and of the system and of sociality) at the expense of the process which then becomes relegated to the sidelines under the heading of madness, holiness or poetry.[28]

To explain the mechanism by which this unity/process relation is played out, Kristeva analyses the process of *signifiance*, the process of production of meaning through the medium of language. Here, the privileged position of the 'unifying instance' is secured by the dominance of what she calls the 'symbolic' over the 'semiotic':

> We shall call *symbolic* the logical and syntactic functioning of language and everything which, in translinguistic practices, is assimilable to the system of language proper. The term *semiotic* on the other hand, will be used to mean: in the first place, what can be hypothetically posited as preceding the imposition of the symbolic via the mirror phase and the acquisition of language, in other words the already given arrangement of the drives in the form of facilitations or pathways; and secondly, the return of these facilitations back into the symbolic system proper, in the form of rhythms, intonations and lexical, syntactic and rhetorical transformations. If the *symbolic* established the limits and the unity of a signifying practice, the *semiotic* registers in that practice the effect of that which cannot be pinned down as sign, whether signifier or signified.[29]

The relation between the symbolic and the semiotic in any signifying practice determines its political significance. Because the force of the symbolic is associated with the maintenance of structures establishing the institutions of the status quo, 'A signifying practice that gives a privileged role to the semiotic process through which the rules of symbolic exchange are redistributed cannot but find itself aligned with political experiences and social movements that contest existing relations of production'[30]

For Kristeva, the 'poetic language' of the literary avant-garde is among the most important of these signifying practices. That avant-garde consists of the authors condemned as 'unreadable' by the cultural institutions of realism, since its work consists in the dissolution of the fixed meanings which constituted the security of realism. Their political efficacy lies in their ability to 'reveal the economic and social formation that shelters them as a provisional articulation, constantly exceeded and threatened by the permanent contradiction proper to the process of *signifiance* — a contradiction between symbolic and semiotic inherent in any speaking being from the moment it speaks to another by means of signs.'[31]

This formulation highlights some of central differences between Kristeva's theory and that of the traditional Marxisms. The promise of semiotics for Marxist aesthetics had been its ability to suggest a radical re-formulation of the theoretical difficulties presented by the base/superstructure model. In Kristeva's words, it is the signifying dimension 'without which no linkages between "base" and "superstructure" can exist'. Both the individual (as subject) and the ideological are constructed in signification, in language. In this region, it will then be possible for an authentic articulation of Freud and Marx to take place.

However, once it is agreed that much of traditional Marxist aesthetics ultimately consigns language and art to a passive, reflectionist position, Kristeva's solution itself is open to a variety of criticisms. The first is signalled by the concept of a 'permanent contradiction' between semiotic and symbolic 'inherent in any speaking being'. Kristeva presents this contradiction as another level to be added to that at which the basic Marxist contradiction between forces and relations of production operates. However, the latter is not permanent — it is resolved through revolution — and nor are its effects similar in 'every speaking being': they are differentiated by the class position of each person.

The permanence of the semiotic/symbolic contradiction suggests that it is constitutive of the human being itself, as is human biology. Such a factor, which is more permanent than a specific class society, then becomes either peripheral to social practice, or is installed at its heart. Human biology or climate have been seen in the

Marxist tradition as peripheral to class struggle since they may determine its limits or shape, but are not active, transformative factors because of their relative permanence. The Freudian factor, however, has often been introduced as a master contradiction, the motor of social change in successive class societies, taking on a different guise at each stage. Such is the nature of Marcuse's argument in *Eros and Civilisation*. Kristeva's theory also seems to tend towards such a position, although she associates the permanence of the semiotic/symbolic contradiction with the continuity of patriarchal structures in successive class societies. Such structures are, for her, inherently bound up with Western systems of signification and production of meaning. Her work *On Chinese Women* (1977) represents an attempt to relate a different system of signification (which involves a different semiotic/symbolic relation) to the problem of destroying patriarchy. It should be noted, though, that there is another position involving feminism, psychoanalysis and Marxism which is sharply critical of Kristeva because she concentrates on individual subjectivity and 'the relativisation of the Symbolic' rather than the struggle for 'a different Symbolic Order other than that consecrated by patriarchy' (Johnston 1976).

Kristeva's theory is vulnerable to a further attack from the standpoint of Marxism for its lack of any reference to class, class position or class ideology as determining factors within a theory of ideology and of aesthetics. The ideological space of the social formation is taken up by the 'mythical' or 'realist' dominant signifying practices which sustain the power of the ruling class, and by the oppositional practice of *écriture*, 'poetic language' and the ascendancy of the semiotic which are, seemingly, de-classed.

The contrast is not simply with the reductionism of socialist realism, but with Gramsci and Althusser. In Gramsci there is, crucially, those contradictory ideologies of the subordinate class, from which elements can be extracted and recombined through the practice of ideological class struggle. In Althusser, the contradictory elements in struggle within the Ideological State Institutions are fuelled 'from outside', from the class struggle between bourgeoisie and proletariat. The work of the *Tel Quel* group has greatly added to the weight of argument against the 'sociological' approach of Plekhanov within Marxist aesthetics, In the process, however, their theory has shown a tendency to move to the opposite pole, where Kristeva's insistence on 'poetic language' and 'the semiotic' often seems to echo the literary politics of the Russian Formalists. Like theirs so often was, the practice of *Tel Quel* too often has seemed to be a reflection or a justification of their theory rather than a concrete application of it in a specific political context.

This last point is reflected in a striking, if only superficial, convergence of the aesthetic politics of the *Tel Quel* group and the Frankfurt School (Adorno and Marcuse). For both, the dominant ideology in art is contested only by certain specified practices of 'avant-garde' art. Both champion these works against all varieties of 'realism', bourgeois or socialist. In the end, both seem more concerned with the subversion of established meaning, than the attempt to go beyond it to create new meanings.

BIBLIOGRAPHICAL NOTE

Sartre's concepts in the *Critique of Dialectical Reason* are discussed by Laing and Cooper (1965), Jameson (1971) and Chiodi (1975). On Lucien Goldmann, see the lengthy introduction to Goldmann (1976) and Glucksmann (1969). Althusser on art is discussed by Barker (1977) and applied by Oakley (1975) and Eagleton (1976a). On Gramsci, see Hall et al. (1977), Anderson (1976-7), Williams (1973) and the standard biography, Fiori (1970). Barthes and *Tel Quel* are discussed in the perspective of the *nouveau roman* by Heath (1972). Kristeva's ideas are expounded in Coward and Ellis (1977), which also provides an introduction to semiotics and to Lacan.

Chapter Six

MARXISM AND POPULAR CULTURE

1. THE CULTURE INDUSTRY

> Even when it is presented in the most banal form, or when it
> glosses over the most profound human problems, concealing their
> underlying and living contradictions, mass art plays a well-
> defined ideological role: to keep mass man in his place, make him
> feel at home in his mass being and close the windows through
> which he might catch a glimpse of a truly human world — and
> with it the possibility of becoming conscious of his alienation as
> well as the means of abolishing it. (Sanchez Vasquez, 1973)[1]

Marxist aesthetics tends to be at its most retarded when
faced with the newer mass cultural forms of the twentieth
century. It thereby betrays its origins in the nineteenth-
century intellectual milieu for which the book was the
model of culture. The book could be apprehended in silent
reflection as the repository of an individual vision, striving
towards that 'intensive totality' prized by Lukacs in great
art. But television programmes, films, records are the
products of a collaboration in which art is indistinguishable
from technology; they are openly and brazenly 'commercial' and 'industrial'; they are immediate and
apparently ephemeral in their impact.

Nevertheless, these forms represent the vast majority of
the cultural material for which the working class of
Western capitalism provide the audience. The choice
before Marxist critics and theorists is either to take them
seriously as cultural forms, applying the same kind of
criteria as they do to the more hallowed arts, or to exclude
them from the aesthetic, seeing them as wholly
'ideological'. With the exception of cinema, which soon
became generally accepted as the 'seventh art', the bulk of

Marxist writing on the mass cultural forms has been hostile. The content and level of these arguments have varied enormously. At one extreme were the official Communist positions during the Cold War era, when the American origins of much popular culture were used as a basis for an attack on cultural imperialism in Western Europe. (Such a slogan has recently been used in Latin America, but with greater justification.) Sanchez Vasquez (1973) launches an abstract attack on the creation of 'mass man', with the main aesthetic objection to mass art emerging as a condemnation of the 'repetition' involved in television, films and music. That observation also occurs in the most developed onslaught on the 'culture industry', that of the Frankfurt School.

The most programmatic statements of the School's position are to be found in *Dialectic of Enlightenment* (Adorno and Horkheimer, 1972) and Herbert Marcuse's *One Dimensional Man*. The first book was originally written in 1944, but the introduction to the English edition does not abandon the general thesis, that the shift towards authoritarianism of a Fascist type was an inevitable feature of capitalism in its monopoly phase. The culture industry is presented as a key institution of this 'administered' society:

> The need which might resist central control has already been suppressed by the control of the individual consciousness. The step from the telephone to the radio has clearly distinguished the roles. The former still allowed the subscriber to play the role of subject and was liberal. The latter is democratic: it turns all participants into listeners and authoritatively subjects them to broadcast programs which are all exactly the same.[2]

This extract illustrates the limits and strengths of a Frankfurt analysis. The dynamic of grand theory leads Adorno and Horkheimer to present a 'step from the telephone to the radio' as if the authoritarian society had *replaced* one by the other, while, in fact, both exist side by side. That unevenness of social development has no place in the grand theory, which consequently has to gloss over it as 'inessential'. The strength of the Frankfurt position is that its argument about the character of the new media is underpinned by a theory of the mechanisms by which they extend 'central control':

> Cartoons were once the exponents of fantasy as opposed to rationalism. They ensured that justice was done to the creatures and objects they electrified, by giving the maimed specimens a second life. All they do today is to confirm the victory of technological reason over truth . . . they hammer into every brain the old lesson that continuous friction, the breaking down of all individual resistance, is the condition of life in this society. Donald Duck in the cartoons and the unfortunate in real life get their thrashing so that the audience can learn to take their own punishment.[3]

The discussion of cartoons introduces the principal mechanism by which the culture industry controls its audience: the Freudian motifs of sadism and masochism. The swift changes of fashion in popular music are explained as a process in which 'likes which have been enforced on listeners provoke revenge the moment the pressure is relaxed. They compensate for their guilt in having condoned the worthless by making fun of it'. Thus, even when criticising the products of the system, the audience remains in its grip.

The Frankfurt analysis is also concerned with the fate of high art in a society dominated by the culture industry. Marcuse devotes a chapter of his book to describing how 'the process of technological rationality is liquidating the oppositional and transcending elements in the 'higher culture'. They succumb in fact to the process of *desublimation* which prevails in the advanced regions of contemporary society'.[4] This process is the result of the diffusion on a massive scale of that higher culture through records, radio and mass produced books. For although this destroys the possession of culture by a social élite, it also destroys what was 'a protected realm in which the tabooed truths could survive in abstract integrity — remote from the society which suppressed them'.[5]

Adorno and Horkheimer go further, by suggesting that the apparent abolition of the commodity form of the play or symphony by their 'free' broadcast on the radio, is a retro-grade step:

> Those who spent their money in the nineteenth or early twentieth century to see a play or go to a concert respected the performance as much as the money they spent. The bourgeois who wanted to get something out of it tried occasionally to establish some rapport with the work . . . Art exercised some restraint on the bourgeois as long as it cost money. That is now a thing of the past. Now that it has lost every restraint and there is no need to pay any money, the proximity of art to those who are exposed to it completes the alienation and assimilates one to the other under the banner of triumphant objectivity.[6]

This passage contains a severely qualified, but also wistful, backward glance to the age of liberal capitalism, before the industrialisation of culture, when art still retained its 'aura'. The term comes from Walter Benjamin's *The Work Of Art In The Age Of Mechanical Reproduction*, an essay in which he evaluates the same phenomena as the Frankfurt authors, but in a diametrically opposed manner.

The aura of a work of art, for Benjamin, is dependent on its 'uniqueness', a property which mechanical reproduction renders obsolete:

> By making many reproductions it substitutes a plurality of copies for a unique existence. And in permitting the reproduction to meet the beholder or listener in his own particular situation, it reactivates the object reproduced. These two processes lead to a tremendous shattering of tradition which is the obverse of the contemporary crisis and renewal of mankind. Both processes are intimately connected with the contemporary mass movements. Their most powerful agent is the film.[7]

Marcuse's 'desublimation' is thus Benjamin's 'shattering of tradition'. The heart of his essay lies in his attempt to show an active link between the proletariat and the new cultural forms. Whereas the Frankfurt analysis places the masses in the role of victims of these forms, for Benjamin the mass is their *subject*, whose emergent needs and modes of perception are matched in the aesthetic procedures of film and gramophone records:

> The mass is a matrix from which all traditional behaviour towards works of art issues today in a new form. Quantity has been

transformed into quality. The greatly increased mass of participation has produced a change in the mode of participation. The fact that the new mode of participation first appeared in a disreputable form must not confuse the spectator . . . Mechanical reproduction of the work of art changes the reaction of the masses towards art. The reactionary attitude towards a Picasso painting changes into the progressive reaction towards a Chaplin movie. The progressive reaction is characterized by the direct, intimate fusion of visual and emotional enjoyment with the orientation of the expert.[8]

Benjamin's work is a quarry of ideas, rather than a coherent general theory. Thus, there is a tendency to 'technological determinism' in the way he describes the new media without commenting on their operation within limits set by capitalism. Similarly, the precise status of the relationship between the proletariat and the mass-media remains obscure. They emerge into history simultaneously, the masses as a political and cultural force (as voters and consumers), the media as structured by their ability to communicate to masses, e.g. to large numbers, but also to a *collective* audience. But these hints also suggest a solution to the problem of determining what the 'relative autonomy' of art might consist of within Marxist theory. For the internal history of the aesthetic level is presented by Benjamin as the result of new technology (mechanical reproduction) making possible new art-forms (cinema) which 'effortlessly' bring to fruition and a mass-audience the innovations of yesterday's avant-garde (Picasso, Dada).

Like the Frankfurt School, Benjamin was keen to specify what tendencies in art were conducive to a Fascist sensibility and which could be the basis of an opposition to it. His own theses, he wrote, 'brush aside a number of outmoded concepts, such as creativity and genius, eternal value and mystery — concepts whose uncontrolled (and at present almost uncontrollable) application would lead to a processing of data in the Fascist sense'.[9]

On reading Benjamin's essay, Adorno was quick to counter-attack. He rejected the total condemnation of the

traditional work of art, since for him it contained its positive 'truth' as well as the aura which represented the
fetishisation of art. And he rejected the polarisation
between these rejected works and Benjamin's wholesale
advocacy of the new forms:

> It would be romantic to sacrifice one to the other, either as the
> bourgeois romanticism of the conservation of personality and all
> that stuff, or as the anarchistic romanticism of blind confidence in
> the spontaneous power of the proletariat in the historical process
> — a proletariat which is itself a product of bourgeois society.[10]

Adorno suggests that Benjamin's work is guilty of the latter
form of romanticism, somewhat unconvincingly citing
Lenin on the need to bring political consciousness to the
proletariat 'from outside'. He also signals the confrontation
between his view and Benjamin's by countering the latter's
description of the 'progressive reaction' with his own
observations of the sado-masochism of cinema audiences.

The most important attempt to get beyond the apparent
deadlock of this confrontation is that of Enzensberger
(1976). Basing his work on elements of Benjamin's ideas,
Enzensberger re-orientates them around a central contradiction, between the forces of production (the forms and
technologies themselves) and the social relations of production (their use and function within capitalist society). Such
a contradiction, which corrects an imbalance in Benjamin's
work, is only occasionally suggested in the earlier writers.
Adorno's concept of radical music does, in fact, adopt these
terms, though that of course is reserved to *avant-garde*
music only. And an embryonic version is to be found in
Benjamin's comments on the capitalist domination of film
and its reactionary attempt to perpetuate the 'aura' of traditional art through the star system.

Enzensberger's essay, written in 1969 is polemical. It is
aimed at Lukacs, the Frankfurt School and their followers
in the German New Left, in whose opposition to the media,
'old bourgeois fears such as the fear of "the masses" seem
to be reappearing along with equally old bourgeois longings
for   pre-industrial   times   dressed   up   in   progressive

clothing'.[11] Following Benjamin, he suggests that traditional art has been 'surpassed' by the new media, so that

> a radical change in perspective is needed. Instead of looking at the
> productions of the new media from the point of view of the older
> modes of production we must, on the contrary, analyse the
> products of the traditional 'artistic media' from the standpoint of
> modern conditions of production.[12]

The place of written culture in an age when 'almost every-
body (including authors) speaks better than he writes' is
considered by Enzensberger, but without any concessions
to 'McLuhan's attempt to stand Marx on his head'. The
unfulfilled potential of the electronic media within
capitalism include their collective character and their
ability to function as genuine two-way communications
media. Enzensberger points out that a radio receiver could
become a transmitter with only the minimum technological
innovation. He also comments on the use of the media by
the masses as instruments of leisure rather than of communication:

> Tape recorders, ordinary cameras, and movie cameras are already
> extensively owned by wage-earners. The question is why these
> means of production do not turn up at factories, in schools, in the
> offices of the bureaucracy, in short, everywhere where there is
> social conflict.[13]

2. TELEVISION AND FILM

Enzensberger's ability to see the electronic media as a
system of cultural forms has not been shared by other
Marxists working on the same area of problems at the level
of theory. There has been very little interaction, for
instance, between film theory (the most developed) and the
study of television. While the former has, in the main,
followed the pattern of the Althusser and *Tel Quel* schools
in searching after the truly adequate theory of ideology and
subjectivity, television has suffered from its 'impurity' as
an artistic form, and the implication that it falls outside the
line of demarcation of the aesthetic. Few Marxists have

followed the host of bourgeois sociologists and social psychologists into a field beset by positivism and behaviourism. Those who have include the *Communications* group in Paris, the Italian semiologist Umberto Eco and Raymond Williams in Britain.[14] Interestingly, none of these studies can be said to be explicitly Marxist in orientation.

Marxist film theory and criticism had a fitful history until after the Second World War. The Hungarian writer Bela Balazs, a contemporary of Lukacs, developed a film aesthetic during the 1920s.[15] For him, the film represented the return of the visual in art after an era dominated by the legible and the audible. Like many other early writers on the cinema Balazs considered that the silent film represented the essence of the form. In the Soviet Union the great directors of the 1920s (Eisenstein, Vertov, Pudovkin) wrote copiously about methods of film production, while the Formalist critic Boris Eikhenbaum anticipated Walter Benjamin's theses in his 'Problems Of Film Stylistics':

> The demand for a new popular art has long been evident — an art whose specific artistic views would be intelligible to the masses, especially the urban masses who do not have their own 'folklore'. This art, as one directed to the masses, had to appear in the category of a new 'primitive', set in revolutionary opposition to the refined forms of the older arts which live a life apart.[16]

Later, Theodor Adorno followed up his debate with Benjamin by collaborating with the German Marxist composer and colleague of Brecht, Hanns Eisler, on a book about film music (Adorno and Eisler, 1947).

The main centres of film theory since 1945 have been France and Italy, the countries which also produced two of the most important schools of European film-making (the *nouvelle vague* and neo-realism). For a considerable period, the 'dominant ideology' in film theory was the realist position associated with André Bazin, a champion of the work of the Italian neo-realists, notably Rossellini. The Soviet *montage* films of Eisenstein and others were rejected as inauthentic, although the Italian Marxist philosopher,

Della Volpe, took a rationalist and modernist position on film in his essay 'Laocoon 1960' (Della Volpe 1960).

The first sustained challenge to Bazin's realism came from semiology, in the work of the French review *Communications* and of Umberto Eco in Italy. They provided accounts of films as constructs rather than as the natural, organic objects of Bazin's theory. Eco (1968) posited ten codes operative in the film, which combine and re-combine to produce the 'natural' image of Bazin's realism. Christian Metz, of *Communications*, proposed the text of the film to be coded at five levels, from that of perception itself to the fundamental filmic codes or conventions which organise the film as a unity.[17]

These analyses were not, in themselves, Marxist. But in their systematic and scientific approach they were seen as coming within the ambiance of the new area of Marxist thought initiated by Althusser. As film critics and film-makers became radicalised in the period before and during the events of May 1968, Metz played the same role for Marxists in film as Barthes had for *Tel Quel*. His work was seen as the basis for a Marxist theory of film as a 'signifying practice'.

This 'Marxist-Leninist' phase was characterised by vigorous polemics between two journals, *Cahiers du Cinéma* (newly radicalised after having been the main bastion of Bazin's position) and *Cinéthique*, which to begin with was allied to *Tel Quel*. Both took as axiomatic the principles of semiotics, but while *Cahiers* emphasised the re-thinking of the history and technology of the cinema,[18] *Cinéthique* placed greater weight on film theory as a guide to the production of the 'revolutionary film'.

Thus, the *Cinéthique* members attempted to 'displace' certain of Metz's theses from his 'pseudo-scientific' problematic to their political one. Metz saw the film as a combination of codes both specific (to the practice of film-making) and non-specific (common to a variety of signifying practices, including politics). Thus, he opposed his theory to the more 'formalist' definitions of film, like Jean-Luc Godard's famous phrase, 'film is images plus sound'. *Cinéthique* took this Metzian idea and politicised it:

> Translating this into Marxist terms, a film is therefore a set of *contradictions* between two types of heterogeneous elements — the specific and non-specific codes — and of contradictions within the specific and within the non-specific codes. These are the contradictions which can be distinguished from the standpoint of ideology. The contradictions which traverse the non-specific codes are in fact those which principally characterise the conflict between bourgeois and proletarian ideologies, investing all the non-specific codes unequally (in their unseparable and unequal relationship) and to varying degrees (in general, the code of dress is less important than the code of speech, but this is not an absolute rule).[19]

Arguing that, in the last instance, the non-specific codes are dominant over the specific (cinematic) ones, *Cinéthique* went on to distinguish between two kinds of 'revolutionary film': the materialist 'deconstruction film' and the Marxist-Leninist political film. The former, favoured by the *Tel Quel* group, was condemned because the attempt to transform the specific, cinematic codes within the film ('deconstruction' of narrative, fixed characters etc.) was not accompanied by a parallel transformation of the non-specific codes. The latter, being dominant, slip back into a non-revolutionary position: "This is subversion — an operation of negation which does not involve the necessity nor the finality of revolutionary politics.' But in the Marxist-Leninist film ('initiated by the work of the Dziga Vertov group'):

> The balance of forces which drives the movement of the film is dictated by the domination of the non-specific codes invested in it. The reason why this system takes in new (specific) codes is because the kind of non-specific (Marxist-Leninist) codes which go to make it up have never (or almost never) featured in what is conventionally known as the History of the Cinema. The novelty of the one summons up the novelty of the other.[20]

The division between 'specific' and 'non-specific' codes is open to criticism as tending to collapse into the traditional separation of art and politics, 'quality' and 'tendency' attacked by Benjamin in 'The Author as Producer'. Nevertheless, the *Cinéthique* view had the virtue of being 'normative' (their term), in linking itself with a contemporary practice of film. The cinema of Godard (with J-L. Gorin the leader of the Dziga Vertov group) is lucidly discussed by Wollen (1972).

The *Cinéthique* position predates the application of Lacanian psychoanalytical notions to the cinema, a process which occurred in France in a parallel way to Kristeva's work associated with literature. Christian Metz led the way in this endeavour, positing a range of concepts which would account for the process of cinema in relation to the Lacanian 'subject', where his earlier theory had dealt only with the internal organisation of the film itself:

> Cinema practice is only possible through the perceptual passions: the desire to see (= scopic drive, scopophilia, voyeurism) acting alone in the art of the silent film, the desire to hear which has been added to it in the sound cinema (this is the *pulsion invocante*, the invocating drive, one of the four main sexual drives for Lacan).[21]

Metz sees the cinema as a crucial 'technique of the imaginary', a term which refers to what Lacan calls the 'mirror phase' of infancy, where 'every other is seen as the same as the subject and difference is not recognised'. In this reading of Lacan, more orthodox than that of Kristeva, the 'imaginary' precedes the 'symbolic' order, which introduces the notions of exclusion and difference. The reference to seeing the other as the same, and its blocking of the recognition of difference, recalls the Brecht, Althusser, Barthes complex of ideas revolving around similar polarities, where the spontaneity and 'natural' character of bourgeois ideology is opposed with various kinds of distanciation devices. One theme in recent film theory has been to try to link up these Marxist positions with Freudian concepts. Metz himself sees the task of the psychoanalytic analysis of cinema to be the disengaging 'of the cinema-object from the imaginary and to win it for the symbolic, in the hope of extending the latter by a new province'.[22]

The theoretical problems posed by any analysis which takes the scientific character of psychoanalysis as given, for a Marxist perspective, are similar in film to those in literature. In one way, they have a more immediate impact, in undercutting that left-wing practice of film which seeks to exhibit militant films in factories and workers' clubs rather than the commercial cinema. For a Lacanian analysis would seem to insist that before the screen, differences of political ideology or class affiliation recede as every spectator is a subject in which the scopic drive predominates.

Nevertheless, the militant political film has undoubtedly been the major achievement of socialist cultural practice in recent years, notably in South America and Western Europe. The American directors like Glauber Rocha (Brazil) and Fernando Solanas (Argentina) make films as part of a revolutionary struggle, 'violent works, made with the camera on one hand and a rock in the other'.[23] In France, the activity of Chris Marker and others has been more in line with Enzensberger's perspectives. Marker equipped workers with 8mm cameras, because:

> The goal was to have the worker film his way of looking at the world, just as if he were writing it. This has opened up unheard of prospects for the cinema; above all a new conception of film making and the significance of art in our time.[24]

3. POPULAR MUSIC

Because nearly all versions of Marxist aesthetics have taken literature as their model, music has posed special problems, and has received little attention. The 'socialist realist' theory of music is almost non-existent, except as a stick with which to beat Soviet composers suspected of modernism. It was probably the most conservative variant of socialist realist theory and, in the Soviet Union, the most clearly nationalistic. According to Schwarz (1972), Zhdanov favoured the continuation of nineteenth century programme music, i.e. orchestral music provided with some underlying idea or story', indicated by a title drawn from literature or history:

> While the popularity of 'programme' music declined sharply in the West during the twentieth century, Soviet theorists and composers continued to cling to the 'pictorialization' of music as a means of making it more accessible. Zhdanov considered the neglect of programme music as a break with the classical heritage, saying that 'the neglect of programme music is also a retreat from progressive traditions. As you know, Russian classical music was, as a rule, programme music.'[25]

Another way in which Soviet composers endeavoured to make their work 'more accessible' was to draw on the traditions of folk music in the various parts of the country. Similarly, the return to folk music sources by Eastern European composers like Bartok and Kodaly was linked with the radical nationalism of the end of the nineteenth century. This strand of cultural activity was inherited by the Communist parties of those countries with a continuing peasant culture, so that folk music as mediated by 'classical' composers became an important component of their socialist music. It is the root, for instance, of the 'Kodaly method' of music teaching in Hungary, where folk songs are the basis of voice training. On the theoretical front, attempts have been made to posit a class basis to the historical division between folk and 'court' music, with the former possessing certain 'collectivist' characteristics from the beginning. (Marothy, 1974)

Folk music was also important for the left in Western countries, as a touchstone for judging 'commercialised' popular music. The American folk song 'revivals' of the 1940s and 1960s were closely linked with left-wing movements, and contained both topical political songs and others whose lineage could be traced to rural communities of blacks or whites in the South. Jazz was more of a borderline case, since it had provided dance rhythms for commercial popular music, but Newton (1959) and Finklestein (1948) were able to present it as a genuine negro folk art, in the latter case drawing clear parallels with East European socialist music which also symphonised folk material.

The problem was, though, that jazz might be 'a people's music', but the music the people actually listened to was something else. Popular music, in general, was excluded from Marxist aesthetic discourse almost totally until the 1960s. The principal exception was Adorno, who paid detailed, if hostile, attention to its workings in *On Popular Music* (1941). Like his other work on the culture industry, this essay contrasted the situation of competitive capitalism with that of the era of monopolies:

> The musical standards of popular music were originally developed by a competitive process. As one particular song scored a great success, hundreds of others sprang up, imitating the successful one . . . Large-scale economic concentration institutionalised the standardisation and made it imperative. As a result innovations by rugged individualists have been outlawed . . .'[26]

Adorno defines this 'standardisation' at the level of theme (love-song, mother-song, nonsense or novelty song, etc.' and that of internal structure. He adopts the 'organic' criterion for great art, where 'the detail virtually contains the whole and leads to the exposition of the whole'. In popular music, the relationship between part and whole is 'fortuitous', 'the composition hears for the listener'. The music is 'pre-digested', although it must be 'pseudo individualised', so that it can be familiar, yet different.

The essay goes on to discuss the mechanisms of promotion and persuasion essential to sell the music to the listener. Here, Adorno returns to his Freudian motifs in describing the modes by which the listener becomes the victim of the industry. The repetition of a song on the radio makes the listener 'enraptured with the inescapable', while the song itself is invested with 'glamour' through 'those in numerable passages in song arrangements which appear to communicate the "now we present" attitude . . . Glamour is made into the eternal conqueror's song of the common man; he who is never permitted to conquer in life, conquers in glamour'.[27]

In Adorno's view, the popular music system acts as a form of 'social cement', bringing the listener more firmly under the domination of an authoritarian society, since:

> The actual function of sentimental music lies in the temporary release given to the awareness that one has missed fulfillment . . . Music that permits its listeners the confession of their unhappiness reconciles them, by means of this 'release' to their social dependence.[28]

Sartre (1976) provides an equally negative view of one aspect of the popular music system, but his concern is to understand the formation of the 'mass public' for hit records as a 'serial' group, standing over against the 'sovereign' group (the recording industry and its satellites, radio, television etc.). A serial group is one whose unity is externally determined — Sartre's well-known example is a bus queue. It contrasts with the 'fused' group, the crowd storming the Bastille or the Winter Palace. In discussing the same phenomenon of the hit record, which Adorno explained through standardisation of the product and the induced subservience of the listener, Sartre borrows an idea from the American sociologist David Riesman:

> The hit record is a record I must have because the Other has it, a record which I will listen to as an Other, adapting my reactions to those which I anticipate in Others.[29]

The value of these studies of popular music lies in their ability to describe the mechanisms by which certain aspects of popular music operate. They also suggest, however, that such is the dominance of those mechanisms that the system is free of contradiction, that here is one place in which any fundamental class or ideological opposition is finally neutralised. While this is the main tenor of Adorno's argument, it is qualified in a footnote which anticipates the later attempts to evaluate some aspects of popular music in a favourable manner:

> The attitude of distraction is not a completely universal one. Particularly youngsters who invest popular music with their own feelings are not yet completely blunted to all its effects. The whole problem of age levels with regard to popular music, however, is beyond the scope of the present study. Demographic problems too must remain out of consideration.

It was precisely these factors — demography (the 'folk-like' music of blacks and rural whites) and youth — which were to be adduced as the main elements of a qualitative change in popular music in the 1950s, through the rise of rock 'n' roll. It was argued that this new genre represented an irruption of these 'authentic' musics into the popular mainstream where they were adopted by a social group-as-audience, teenagers, whose specific needs were previously neglected by that mainstream. The standard history of rock 'n' roll (Gillett, 1969) located the economic base of this development in a resurgence of entrepreneurial organisations within popular music, challenging the control of centralised entertainment corporations of the type which Adorno's account had considered to be totally triumphant.

During the 1960s, radical and Marxist considerations of popular music tended to be of a sociological type, including at least one attempt to theorise 'youth' as a new proletariat (Rowntree and Rowntree, 1968). In reaction to such exotic responses to the 'youth revolt' and 'counter culture', there was a swing back amongst British Marxist authors to a more traditional class analysis of the popular culture of the era. A representative text is *Resistance Through Rituals* (eds. Hall and Jefferson, 1976), where a theory of 'sub-cultures' is developed using elements of Gramsci's theory of hegemony and Althusser's concept of ideology. The apparently 'classless' sub-cultures of the 1960s are shown to embody traditional working-class themes and to represent an 'imaginary solution to real problems'.

In all this, popular music itself was seldom granted a

'relative autonomy' from the sub-culture by which it was adopted. Elsewhere there were tentative attempts to discover in what this autonomy might consist, including one suggestion that Adorno's polarity between Schonberg and Stravinsky might be applied to the Rolling Stones and the Beatles (Merton, 1968), and another that semiotics might fruitfully be applied to the analysis of the internal structure of the music (Laing, 1969). A more extended attempt to evolve a specific Marxist aesthetic of music was provided by Carles and Comolli (1971). This examination of black American free jazz was based broadly on that modernist (Althusser/Barthes) Marxist aesthetic which regards the deconstruction of 'finished' artistic modes as a primary aim of progressive art. Thus 'free jazz', the product of the historical situation of black americans, exposed the 'ecumenical' myth of jazz as a harmonious unity of disparate elements, just as 'black power' exposed the myth of America as a similar harmonious unity.

Chapter Seven

BRITISH AND AMERICAN DEVELOPMENTS

1. ROMANTICISM AND MARXISM

THE growth of Marxism in Britain (or the lack of it) was one aspect of a major debate between Perry Anderson and E. P. Thompson in 1965-7 concerning recent British history and its political implications.[1] In reply to the assertions by Anderson and Tom Nairn that there was no British Marxist tradition comparable to those of France, Germany or Italy, Thompson stated that; 'As a pattern of attraction and repulsion, Marxism and anti-Marxism permeates our culture.'[2] Yet, whatever the strength of 'anti-Marxism' in the Anglo-Saxon countries, the evidence seems to suggest that whatever its quantity at certain times (notably the 1930s), Marxism has produced little work of outstanding originality in Britain and America. The one exception is in the various branches of history, where the books of Thompson himself, Christopher Hill, E. J. Hobsbawm, Eugene Genovese, Joseph Needham and others have made a major impact.

Most Marxist attempts to explain this lack have been subjective, diagnosing a 'failure' of the Anglo-Saxon Left to establish itself. But Anderson and Nairn have tried to situate this failure in structural terms. Nairn (1965) gave two reasons: first, that the Marxism of the 1880s, when the first British socialist group was established, was not sophisticated enough at the level of 'examination of the superstructures', and secondly, the 'nullity of native intellectual traditions' did not provide a fertile mental environment for Marxism to develop, in contrast to German classical philosophy.

122

The second part of the argument was elaborated by Anderson (1969). British intellectual life was said to have an 'absent centre', in its lack of a classical sociology able to conceive of society as a totality and therefore able to provide a locus for the growth of an indigenous Marxism. Instead, the role of a 'totalising' discipline was taken up by literary studies and the peculiar form of social criticism associated with it, the tradition studied in Raymond Williams' *Culture and Society* (1958). That work and its successor (*The Long Revolution*, 1960) marked, in fact, the apex of the 'social criticism' tradition and the beginning of its confrontation with Marxism in Williams' writings, a point which will be explored later in this chapter.

If Anderson's argument is not sufficient to explain the paucity of Marxist thought in Britain in its entirety, it immediately throws light on the fact that the first English Marxist of any stature was an artist, who came to socialism through that 'social criticism' tradition. Unlike the process elsewhere, in which aesthetics generally entered a national Marxism at a relatively late stage, William Morris' inheritance of an aesthetic critique of industrial capitalism enabled him to embrace Marxism as a logical extension of the social criticism of Ruskin and Carlyle.

Born in 1834, Morris was in his forties when he became a socialist. As a Pre-Raphaelite artist, he had shared in the criticism of capitalism levelled by Ruskin and others, in which the criterion of excellence was the idealised craftsmanship of the mediaeval period. As a designer and painter, Morris had tried to create works in the spirit, which would stand in opposition to the ugliness of capitalist production. It was an inadequate solution, and in socialism Morris discovered the means by which the question of beauty could be resolved in a political manner, through the revolution. With Eleanor Marx and Edward Aveling, he was a founder member of the Socialist League in 1884. His famous 'utopian' novel, *News from Nowhere*, was first published in the League's journal, probably as a rebuttal of an American bourgeois vision of the future, Bellamy's *Looking Backward*.[3]

Although Morris's revolutionary commitment is undoubted, Marxist accounts of his ideas differ widely. In the second edition of his standard biography of Morris, E. P. Thompson argues that the attempt to fit Morris into a Marxist or anti-Marxist schema entails the repression of important aspects of his work. In Thompson's view Morris represents a fruitful meeting-point of Romantic and Marxist thought.

Two aspects of Morris' ideas made significant contributions to a Marxist aesthetic: his re-definition of the concept of art, and the 'utopianism' of his fictional works. Rejecting any separation between objects of beauty and objects of utility, he gave art a social and political dimension:

> To a socialist a house, a knife, a cup, a steam engine, or what not, anything, I repeat that is made by man and has form, must either be a work of art of destructive of art. The Commercialist, on the other hand, divides 'manufactured articles' into those which are prepensely works of art, and are offered for sale in the market as such, and those which have no pretence and could have no pretence to artistic qualities.[4]

Since Engels' *Socialism, Utopian and Scientific* (1880), a clear line has been drawn between the politics of Marxism and that of 'utopian socialism', principally because the latter neglected the key issue of the means by which the transition to socialism was to occur. William Morris' utopian writings, however, were produced in harness with what he called his work as a 'practical socialist'. Speculation about the future was, in any case, an accepted part of Marxist propaganda work: the German Marxist August Bebel wrote a pamphlet entitled *The Society of the Future*.

Nevertheless, Morris' work has been criticised for a certain regression towards the mediaevalism of the Pre-Raphaelites in his vision of the future. Williams (1958) found this to be a distraction from the political essays and lectures he regarded as the essential Morris. Others have compared it to Marx's few comments on the shape of a communist society and found it wanting. Thompson's conclusions, following recent French work on Morris, are that the utopian writings are at a different level to the political theory of the essays. They represent an 'education of desire' for socialist militants, and performed an immediate political function in differentiating genuine revolutionary aims from the State Socialism of the Fabians (Thompson, 1977).

At present, Morris' work remains that of an isolated pioneer within British Marxism and Marxist aesthetics. Any revaluation of his contribution would probably come, as Solomon (1974) argues, from a more general recognition of the importance of a utopian dimension in Marxist thought as a whole. In Britain, however, Morris had little impact in the period before 1939, when Marxism gained a foothold amongst the country's intelligentsia. He was mentioned with approval in John Strachey's influential *Theory and Practice of Socialism* (1936), though the author was most impressed with the chapter in *News From Nowhere* in which Morris describes the 'Great Change', the process of revolution itself, rather than the utopian vision of the remainder of the book.

2. CAUDWELL AND THE THIRTIES

There was, in this period, a large amount of cultural criticism and theoretical work produced in Britain and America, but little matched up to the successes of the political literature of the period. In Britain, three figures stood out: Robert Tressall, Hugh MacDiarmid and Lewis Grassic Gibbon. Unlike the more fêted group of Auden, Spender and Day Lewis, each chose a style and form outside the mainstream of English literary tradition, in order to express meanings which were also alien to the liberalism and conservatism of the English novel and twentieth-century poetry.

If there is such a genre as the 'proletarian novel', Tressall's *The Ragged Trousered Philanthropists* is the paradigmatic example in English. By the standards of classic realism, the narrative is fitful and the characterisation perfunctory, because both are subservient to Tressall's intention of explaining the process of capital's exploitation of labour in a fictional form that is humorous, entertaining and easily accessible for a working-class audience. It stands as a lonely eminence amidst English fiction, although Tressall's modern heirs are undoubtedly the socialist theatre groups whose dramas at their best have a similar momentum.

MacDiarmid and Gibbon were Scots, and wrote out of a consciousness of a distant Scottish radical tradition associated with Robert Burns and others. MacDiarmid's early lyrics had the same directness as those of Burns, while his *Three Hymns To Lenin* represent an effortless expression of political ideas in poetry. Like MacDiarmid, Lewis Grassic Gibbon wrote his trilogy, A *Scots Quair* in a style mixing Scots dialect language with English. The novel is a Scottish equivalent to the epics of socialist realism which represent the peak of Soviet fiction. The three volumes follow the heroine from the countryside to an industrial town to the capital city.

These writers received surprisingly little attention from the Marxist intelligensia during the 1930s. The impact of the latter on British cultural life was, however, substantial through journals like the *Calendar Of Modern Letters* and *Left Review*, while Ralph Fox's *The Novel and the People* was only one of many books of Marxist cultural criticism of the period. Yet the theoretical resources of much of this work was slender. Lukacs was unknown in Britain, and the principal influences were Plekhanov and the current theorists of Soviet socialist realism. As a result, according to Mulhern (1974):

> Literary criticism came to be regarded as the elucidation of the
> social determinations of a text, as the identification of the 'social

equivalent' of a given character, sentiment or situation. There was also a common limitation: although this criticism was newly sociological and political, no profound redefinition of literature was implied. Literature was a datum: only interpretation and judgment were controversial.

There were few exceptions to this tendency. The most important was Christopher Caudwell, whose Marxist writing was done in only two years, 1934-6. He was killed fighting in Spain a year later. Unlike the Oxford and Cambridge educated Marxist intellectuals who dominated communist cultural work in Britain, Caudwell was an autodidact. He therefore drew on a much wider range of sources for his ideas, many of them scientific and anthropological. He also proposed a more ambitious approach to the arts than other British Marxists. In addition to the interpretation of sociological equivalents, he wanted to define the specificity of art as a social practice, in his major work *Illusion and Reality* (1937).

The book was unusual in two respects: in contrast to the many Marxists who assumed literature to mean the novel, Caudwell focused on poetry, and in order to determine the function of poetry, which he assumed to be constant, he sought its origins in primitive societies. His major forerunner in this respect had been Plekhanov, while later authors undertaking a similar task have included George Thomson (in his studies of Greek drama) and Lukacs, in his late aesthetic theory.

Like other writers, Caudwell argued that pre-class societies had a unity of social practice which separated out into the division of labour as class societies developed. Tribal poetry is thus closely linked with the economic and social life of the tribe:

> It expresses the social relation of man's instincts to the ungathered fruit. These instincts have generated these emotions (the emotions present in the poem) just because they have not blindly followed the necessities of the germ plasm, but have been moulded by the objective necessities of collective action to a common economic end. The phantasy of poetry is a social image.[5]

This linking of the biological, psychological, social and natural to form a poetics, is representative of Caudwell's method. The book goes on to trace the separation of poetry from religion, and of science from magic, as class differentiation develops. Nevertheless, poetry retains a necessary role in the relationship of the instincts to social life, and of man to nature. Only the content of the relationships change throughout history.

Poetry thus takes on a privileged status in relation to the other arts:

> Poetry expresses the freedom which inheres in man's general timeless unity in society; it is interested in society as the sum and guardian of common instinctive tendencies; it speaks of love, death, hope, sorrow and despair as all men experience them. The novel is the expression of that freedom which men seek, not in their unity in society but in their differences, of their search for freedom in the pores of society, and therefore of their repulsions from, clashes with, and concrete motions against *other* individuals different from themselves.[6]

The implication is that poetry preserves an essence of humanity, while the novel is a product of class (bourgeois) society and may die with it. This absolute distinction between the poetic essence and the historical shapes it assumes, is perhaps what makes the historical part of *Illusion and Reality* mundane in comparison with its general theory. Caudwell's hectic account of 'capitalist poetry' introduces the single ideological theme which for him characterises bourgeois civilisation: an obsession with 'freedom', which links the philosophy, science and art of the capitalist class in his *Studies In A Dying Culture* (1938). The *locus classicus* for this view is the *Communist Manifesto* where the 'freedom' of the market place is shown to give rise to an increasingly unfree society. Thus:

> The bourgeois poet sees himself as an individualist striving to realise what is most essentially himself by an expansive outward movement of the energy of his heart, by a release of internal forces which outward forms are crippling. This is the bourgeois dream, the dream of one man alone producing the phenomena of the

world. He is Faust, Hamlet, Robinson Crusoe, Satan and Pru-
frock.[7]

But the limitations of this kind of analysis are the limits
of the Marxism of the 1930s. The important side of
Caudwell's work is that which explores the work of poetry,
its means and methods of effectivity. Although dissociating
his ideas from Freud (who was a peddler of the bourgeois
illusion of 'freedom'), Caudwell entitled a chapter of
Illusion and Reality, 'Poetry's Dream-Work', anticipating
much later work on a materialist poetics.

3. SOME AMERICAN THEMES

If the USA did not produce a Caudwell in the 1930s, its
Marxist culture was more vigorous than the more
academically inclined British Marxism. There was a
greater internationalism, principally because American
Marxism took root at first among German and Jewish first
or second generation Americans. The Critics Group in
New York kept abreast of Soviet scholarship and debates,
translating and publishing Lifshitz's study of Marx's
aesthetics and important articles on questions like the
existence of absolute criteria in judging art-works.

American communism produced its share of 'sociological
equivalent' literary criticism in books like Granville Hicks'
Great Tradition (1933) and V. F. Calverton's *Liberation of
American Literature* (1932). There was also a larger group
of writers whose work was, for a while, influenced by the
presence of Marxism in the intellectual milieux of the
Depression and the New Deal. Among them were Edmund
Wilson, John Dos Passos and James T. Farrell. The latter's
essays made use of a sensitive kind of 'neo-Marxism', in for
instance his handling of class analysis in the study of 'Social
Themes in American Realism' (Farrell, 1964). A later writer
with a similar relation to Marxism was Norman Mailer.
His novel *Barbary Shore* was set against a background of
Stalinist-Trotskyist factional fights, while *Advertisements*

for Myself (1959) contained a brief excursion into Marxist theory, 'From Surplus Value to the Mass Media'.

The best communist writing was probably in the field of literary journalism and reportage. Joseph Freeman's auto-biographical *An American Testament* (1938) provides a detailed picture of the writers grouped around the influential journal, *New Masses*, whose mentor had been John Reed, author of *Ten Days That Shook The World*. Solomon (1973) argues that the most original literary theory and criticism was produced by lesser-known figures in the universities and in journals like *Modern Monthly*, now buried in the archives.

In the immediate post-war period, before the stranglehold of McCarthyism virtually silenced American Marxism for nearly a decade, Sidney Finklestein produced a series of books that laid out with clarity a Marxist aesthetic that was both attentive to the details of American culture and remained congruent with orthodox socialist realism. Much of his work dealt with music, both Western classical and jazz, and he was able to show how the best of each was at root 'people's music', because of its origins in folk culture. The further music strayed from such roots, or from the 'programme' genre, it lost vitality, whether in the factory-produced pop song, obscure modernism or Kurt Weill's attitude to jazz as 'bourgeois music' which led him to treat it with 'Expressionistic irony' (Finklestein, 1948). The tone of Finklestein's writing is that of a genial populism, in which American 'democratic traditions' are invoked and to which such notions as 'ideological struggle' would be alien.

The American New Left of the 1960s did not immediately inspire a resurgence of Marxism. Its early temper was determinedly anti-theoretical and tended to associate Marxism with the rigidity of its principal exponents, the Old Left of Communist and Trotskyist parties. This emphasis on the practice of radicalism has carried over into the various radical scholars' movements, which aim more at the transformation of the process of literary education or the theatre than the production of theoretical perspectives. In a declaration on theatre as politics Lee Baxandall states that 'the human aesthetic capacities shall no longer be relegated chiefly to the Other world of the stage play, artwork, poem, novel, etc. . . . Our lives are impoverished of the aesthetic qualities of rhythm and grace and harmony. We are sick for the lack of coherence and intensity of expression. What we want — and a return to the drawbacks of "primitive society" is not necessary, of course — is the integration of the aesthetic with man's other capacities.'[8]

The theoretical bias of American Marxist aesthetics in recent years has tended towards the traditions of the Frankfurt School. The standard history of the School was written by an American (Jay, 1973), while the most persuasive account of 'Hegelian' Marxism is also American (Jameson, 1971). The focal point of this tendency is the journal *Telos*, published in St Louis, and this orientation is reflected to some extent in *Praxis*, a publication aiming to develop 'radical perspectives in the arts'. Finally, the USA has produced the most ambitious attempt to document the history of Marxist aesthetics in the announced twelve-volume series of 'Documents On Marxist Aesthetics' edited by Lee Baxandall and Stefan Morawski, whose selection of Marx and Engels *On Literature and Art* (Marx and Engels, 1973) is the first to be published.

4. NEW DIRECTIONS IN BRITISH MARXISM

The watershed in British Marxism since the Second World War was 1956, when the Hungarian revolt detached a large section of Marxist intellectuals from the Communist Party, and from its orthodox theory, in the formation of the 'New Left'. An orthodox tradition still persisted however, particularly in aesthetics (predominantly literature), mainly because it was already closely linked with the main lines of academic work in Britain.

Like the literary critics of 1930s' Marxism, this tradition lacked any redefinition of literature as an institution. The given limits of 'author' and 'work' were accepted, and Marxist interpretations were offered of the same objects given liberal or conservative approval by bourgeois critics. Thus Arnold Kettle's *An Introduction To The English Novel*, the centrepiece of this trend, mentions Robert Tressall and Lewis Grassic Gibbon as having written 'important and moving novels which have to be seen in their historical context as the beginning of something new in our literature'. However, Kettle does not discuss these working-class novels because 'simply to include one or two of them alongside a totally different type of writing would be satisfactory from no point of view'.[9] There is no recognition of the fact that such books might implicitly challenge the whole ethos of the bourgeois humanist tradition which Kettle's book is concerned to validate through gentle criticism. His work, and that of younger critics, has become the left-wing of orthodox 'non-political' literary studies, rather than achieving a clear break from them.

Alongside this conservative tradition of Marxist work in the 1950s and early 1960s were two significant individual figures, both working at the limits of unsatisfactory traditions, in Marxist and non-Marxist aesthetics and cultural theory. John Berger was a Marxist painter, novelist and critic, concentrating on that point in orthodox socialist realist theory at which the drawbridge came down: its rejection of virtually the whole modern movement in painting and sculpture. Raymond Williams, coming from within the conventional tradition of literary and social criticism, found the pressure of his socialist politics a critical factor in going beyond the tradition, into a space where the available orthodox marxism was seen to be inadequate to answer the questions put to it from Williams' own perspective.

Berger's first collection of essays, *Permanent Red* (Berger, 1960), drew up lists of 'artists defeated by the difficulties', 'artists who struggle' and 'twentieth-century masters' (Gris,

Picasso, Lifshitz, Zadkine and Leger, Berger's prototype of the socialist artist). In this book, Berger had worked through to his own 'revisionist' concept of realism, which was reminiscent of Brecht's repudiation of the Lukacsian insistence of purely aesthetic criteria in defining the concept: 'The only thing shared by all Realists is the nature of their relationship to the artistic tradition they inherit. They are Realists in so far as they bring into art aspects of nature and life previously ignored or forbidden by the rule-makers.'[10] A remark about Picasso suggested the originality of Berger's approach:

> The critical minority in the Communist Party take him too seriously because they consider him capable of being a great socialist artist and assume his political allegiance is the result of dialectical thinking rather than of a revolutionary instinct.[11]

That insight was to be developed in Berger's *Success and Failure of Picasso* (1965), while the essay 'The Moment of Cubism' placed that artistic school in a complex of revolutionary developments across European society in the decade 1910-20.

Berger's position was already converging on that of Walter Benjamin in 'The Work of Art in the Age of Mechanical Reproduction' and he explicitly referred to Benjamin's ideas in his *Selected Essays* (1974) and in *Ways of Seeing* (1972). These books, and his parallel work in fiction and his original form of political documentary writing, found Berger moving beyond the confines of art criticism. *Ways of Seeing* is remarkable for its demystification of the idea of 'art' itself, something Marxist critics in other aesthetic spheres have often failed to do:

> The uniqueness of every painting was once a part of the uniqueness of the place where it resided. Sometimes the painting was transportable. But it could never be seen in two places at the same time. When the camera reproduces a painting, it destroys the uniqueness of its image. As a result, its meaning changes. Or, more exactly, its meaning multiplies and fragments into many meanings.[12]

Elsewhere in the book Berger extends this critique of the

mythology of art by showing a connection between the presentation of women as objects of possession in oil painting and in modern glamour photography and advertising images. Here, a certain debt to the phenomenological mode of analysis of Sartre in his *Critique* is apparent:

> The spectator-buyer is meant to envy herself as she will become if she buys the product. She is meant to imagine herself transformed by the product into an object of envy for others, an envy which will then justify her loving herself. One could put this another way: the publicity image steals her love of herself as she is and offers it back to her for the price of the product.[13]

This mode of observation is also a component of the two books on which Berger collaborated with photographer Jean Mohr. *A Fortunate Man* (1967) and *A Seventh Man* (1975) represent an attempt to transcend the boundaries between the *genres* of biography and documentary, the subjective and the objective. In each, the writing acts as a mediation between the inner world of a country doctor and an immigrant worker and the objective conditions which shape its contours. In this practice, too, Berger is a disciple of Benjamin, since the books represent that 'functional transformation of forms and instruments of production by a progressive intelligentsia', that is the political task of the author as producer.

Raymond Williams, like John Berger, is an isolated figure in British cultural life as a whole, and within its Marxist segment. Although Williams has published a dozen books in nearly twenty years it was not until 1976 that Eagleton's *Literature and Ideology* made the first Marxist critique of his work since E. P. Thompson's searching review of *The Long Revolution* in 1960. The isolation of such an important body of writing is only in part due to much of it being produced under the sign of literary criticism. It is also the result of that lack of a thriving British Marxist culture noted by Perry Anderson.

In the introduction to *Marxism and Literature* (1977)

Williams for the first time places his work within Marxism, describing it as a 'cultural materialism'. In doing so, he explains that ever since the 1940s he had been operating in a dialogue, explicit or implicit, with Marxism. But whereas the early years of this period found his inherited social criticism confronted by the monolithic Marxism of an anglicised version of Soviet theory, after 1956 and the birth of the New Left

> I felt the excitement of contact with more new Marxist work: the later work of Lukacs, the later work of Sartre, the developing work of Goldmann and Althusser, the variable and developing syntheses of Marxism and some forms of structuralism. At the same time, within this significant new activity, there was further access to older work, notably that of the Frankfurt School (in its most significant period of the twenties and thirties) and especially the work of Walter Benjamin; the extraordinarily original work of Antonio Gramsci; and, as a decisive element of a new sense of the tradition, newly translated work of Marx and especially the *Grundrisse.*[14]

The main channel for this 'new sense of the tradition' in the English-speaking world has been the journal, *New Left Review.* Beginning in 1957 as the organ of a group of mainly ex-Communist intellectuals, it was a focus both of a re-thinking of Marxism after Hungary and, for a while, of a putative political movement based in a network of 'Left Clubs' and the burgeoning nuclear disarmament movement.

By the early 1960s, a second generation of the New Left dominated the journal. Their priorities were to become those suggested by the magazine's editor, Perry Anderson, to assist in the development of a British Marxism, by disseminating and applying the ideas of those figures of 'Western Marxism' ignored by Soviet orthodoxy (those very figures listed by Raymond Williams above).

The general importance of this 'Western Marxism' for Raymond Williams' approach was that, in a variety of ways, it provided an advance on a Marxism whose practical results in the aesthetic field had seemed to resolve itself into a reduction of works of art to their sociological origins. Now, Goldmann's 'homology', Gramsci's 'hegemony' and Benjamin's notion of art as production suggested that the master-concept of Williams' work, culture, could be given a new, fuller, meaning.

'The concept of "culture" ', he wrote, 'when it is seen in the broad context of historical development, exerts a strong pressure against the limited terms of all the other concepts. That is always its advantage; it is also always the source of its difficulties, both in definition and comprehension.'[15] Terry Eagleton's critique of Williams argued that these 'difficulties' were of Williams' own making, since the concept of 'culture' has no valid Marxist anchorage. According to Eagleton, this concept effectively defuses the concept of 'ideology', which he uses in an Althusserian sense (Eagleton, 1976).

Yet to point to this 'culturalism' of Williams' work is not all there is to be said about it. For what the notion of 'culture' preserves, despite its ambiguity, is the idea of an interconnected ensemble of social practices, aesthetic and others, with an historical dimension. In contrast, Eagleton's own position seems to straddle uneasily the gap between a general concept of ideology as the content of all social practices and the local area of 'literature', which seems to be defined in a very traditional manner as the conventional string of 'great works'.

In its 'practical state' Williams' work has provided valuable analyses of specific instances. His book on *Television* (1974) and the study of George Orwell (1971) are examples. The latter is particularly impressive for the cool way in which Williams disengages a deeply contradictory body of work from the mythological status it has enjoyed within the dominant liberal ideology in Britain. In a sense the importance of *Marxism and Literature*, the close of a long phase in William's work, lies in its attempt to produce a theoretical perspective consonant with the best of his practice. It may well herald a greater influence for Williams mongst those sections of Marxist cultural activity in Britain, where the particular problems of the national ulture are recognised as paramount. There is a parallel to e drawn here with the example of Gramsci's 'cultural' heory. 'In a sense,' writes one of his translators, 'all the Prison] Notebooks can be interpreted as being about ulture — in the sense, that is, of the way life is lived or of vays in which certain concepts come to inform the thinking f various social groups' (Nowell-Smith, 1977). And as Gramsci's investigations are of the forms and processes of talian culture, so Williams' achievement is to have xplored the complexity of British cultural forms and ractices more deeply than any other writer.

If 1956 and after produced a break with older ideas for oth Williams and Berger, the political and theoretical erment of Europe in the late 1960s have also inspired the ewest developments in British Marxist cultural activity. Three instances of these developments seem, in 1977, to be specially significant. The first represents probably the most developed body of socialist practice in the arts, the alternative theatre' movement. It was a product of that ayer of intellectuals and students radicalised by the Paris of May 1968 as well as by the international student 'revolt' nd by the obvious political nullity of both State and rivate sectors of the theatre. In America that side of *avant-arde* theatre associated with 'happenings' seemed to pre-ominate, but in Britain an orientation towards working-lass audiences posed productive questions of style and rm for the new theatre groups.

The important articles by John McGrath (of the 7:84 roup) and Richard Seyd (*Red Ladder*) spell out the way in hich politics and aesthetics have been intertwined in deal-g with issues like the use of popular cultural material as w material for political argument, and the nature and gnificance of genuinely collective work (McGrath, 1975; eyd, 1975). Ironically, perhaps, the achievements of this eatre (and of television writers and directors like Trevor

Griffiths, Jim Allen and Ken Loach) has received only
cursory attention from Marxists working on problems of
theory and analysis in art and culture. It still lacks a critical
attention in depth of the kind Brecht received from
Benjamin and Barthes.

Among those Marxists working on theoretical questions
are the two parallel but contrasting groups associated with
the film theory journal *Screen* and with the Centre for Con
temporary Cultural Studies at Birmingham University
The CCCS was founded by Richard Hoggart, author of
The Uses of Literacy, a pioneering ethnography of English
working-class culture, and most prominent amongst its sub
sequent projects has been the series of studies collected in
Resistance Through Rituals (eds. Hall and Jefferson, 1976)
These studies, to some degree, examine the same terrain as
Hoggart's work, although some twenty-five years on, and
with different theoretical approaches.

The activity of the *Screen* group, on the other hand, has
been concerned with replacing the impressionistic style of
film criticism with the production of a theory of cinema
whose implications carry into the wider sphere of popular
culture, ideology, or signifying practices in general. Since
about 1970, the journal has undergone a change of
emphasis, shedding the 'populism' of an old New Left
approach which undertook to defend the mass-appeal
Hollywood film as worthy of critical attention, in the face
of condemnations from conservative and progressive
opinion alike.

The subsequent evolution of *Screen* closely followed that
of the French groups associated with *Tel Quel* and *Cahier
du Cinema*. A reconsideration of naïve notions of 'realism'
in the cinema was undertaken with ideas introduced by
Russian formalism. Brecht's artistic theory was presented
as an active intervention against naïve realism. Finally
through the work of Metz, Kristeva and the editors of
Cahiers, *Screen* began to work towards a theory of film unit
ing the perspectives of Marx (via *Tel Quel*) and Freud (via

_acan), under the banner of 'materialism'.

Screen, like CCCS although less directly, is part of an
educational institution, the Society for Education in Film
and Television. This situation may have some bearing on
the journal's occasional tendency to seem to be motivated
by a search for a purity of knowledge or 'discourse', rather
than any more directly political aim. However, its most
recent attempts to parallel Kristeva in developing a theory
of ideology dependent on psychoanalytical concepts, has
been explicitly placed in a more general context through a
critique of the *Resistance Through Rituals* text (Coward,
1977).

In one sense, that text is a riposte to Hoggart, and to
those who saw the 'youth culture' of the 1960s as hopelessly commercialised or impressively classless, or both.
Hoggart saw the disintegration of a traditional working-
class way of life, in the face of a cleverly-manipulated commercial culture able to 'mimic' the authentic proletarian
one. The CCCS group took issue both with that view and
with the enthusiasts for 'youth culture' by portraying the
various youth sub-cultures of the 1960s as both 'self-
created' and class-bound, a construction of meanings by
working-class youth out of the cultural commodities of
capitalism, meanings which related to traditional working-
class concerns as 'imaginary solutions to real problems'.

Certain specific difficulties with this work – its tendency
to make cultural artefacts epiphenomena of the sub-cultural
meaning system – have been signalled in the discussion of
popular music in the previous chapter. The critique by
Rosalind Coward in *Screen* is more wide-ranging, accusing
the CCCS group of an 'idealism' in which ideological
practices have no significance apart from their expression
of a class essence, one sign of which is their retention of a
concept of 'culture' as 'the forms in which the groups
handle" the raw material of their social and material existence'.

The critique is similar in direction to the challenge

offered to traditional versions of Marxism by other approaches informed by a semiotics which undertakes to undermine the assumptions of a 'realist' or 'reflectionist' aesthetic. It also points to a definite problem in the way *Resistance Through Rituals* handles the classical issue of the 'relative autonomy' of superstructure from economic base. However, Coward then seems to put forward a Lacanian notion of ideology in such a way that any correspondence, however mediated, between ideological or cultural practices and class positions or subjects, is inadmissible:

> Ideology in this context could be implicitly understood as a system of representations dependent on a certain subject position, constructed by signifying practices. In so far as the signified, the represented, only exists as it is produced in signification, this development of theory no longer need look for a simple relation between the conditions of existence of the means of representation (economic and political determinants) and what is produced by the activity of these means. But this movement away from a 'represented exterior' of signifying practices towards a notion of the inscription of a subject position leaves the theory empty of any easy way of accounting for these representations in terms of a class analysis.[16]

The last statement recognises in a candid way, the inherent difficulty of integrating such a thorough-going adoption of a Lacanian theory with any of the various Marxist definitions of the *relative* autonomy of artistic practices, whether they are considered as 'signifying', 'ideological' or 'expressive'. At this stage of its development, the theory seems to have constructed an object fully autonomous from any external determination, but also fully determining its own effects on the recipient of its significations, the 'subject position constructed by signifying practices'.

It is tempting to try to situate the deadlock between this kind of theorising and that represented by *Resistance Through Rituals* by a resort to a very ancient Marxist procedure, reading off the theory produced from the class-position of its producers. Such an analysis would see the CCCS group, like Richard Hoggart, as 'scholarship boys', detached from their working-class origins by a meritocratic education system, yet eager to insist, in the face of a dominant ideology of a growing 'classlessness' that the proletariat still *exists* as a unified social group, fully differentiated through 'culture' from other classes. *Screen*, in contrast, would be characterised as quintessentially *petit-bourgeois*, driven to insist on the independent role of the members of that class as producers and theorists of cinematic images, immune from that pressure of the class-struggle between proletariat and bourgeoisie that classical Marxism states to be its inevitable condition of existence.

But a more productive perspective on the current state of Marxist aesthetics in Britain, and throughout the capitalist world would have to start by acknowledging that the most politically effective interventions and innovations in the field have been those which have made a rendezvous with a certain practice of art, which have illuminated the field of possibilities for socialist artists and for socialist movements for whom art is, in Mao's formulation, a necessary, if not the most important, part of their struggle. The Marxist theory of art is today immeasurably richer in resources than it was a few decades ago. But a theory which cannot guide practice risks a descent into academic contemplation, just as a practice proud of its spontaneity will often find itself a prisoner of the very ideology it set out to oppose.

FOOTNOTES

Notes to Chapter One

1. Lukacs (1972a) p. 47.
2. *ibid* p. 49.
3. Marx & Engels (1973) pp. 7-8.
4. Quoted in Lifshitz (1973) p. 35.
5. *Ibid* p. 38.
6. Marx & Engels *op. cit.* p. 61.
7. *ibid* p. 52.
8. *ibid* p. 105.
9. *ibid* p. 78.
10. Marx & Engels (1956) p. 102.
11. Marx & Engels (1973) p. 71.
12. *ibid* pp. 80-2.
13. *ibid* p. 85.
14. *ibid* p. 121.
15. Jameson (1971) p. 193.
16. Marx & Engels (1973) p. 145.
17. *ibid* p. 137.
18. Marx, *Theories of Surplus Value* (Moscow, 1963) p. 405. Quoted in Solomon (1974) p. 74.
19. *ibid* p. 401. Quoted in Solomon (1974) p. 75.
20. e.g. to J. Bloch (1890), F. Mehring (1893), F. Starkenberg (1894) W. Borgius (1894). In Marx & Engels (1965).
21. Marx & Engels (1973) p. 89.
22. *ibid* p. 115.
23. Labriola (1908). Quoted in Timpanero (1974) p. 18.
24. Plekhanov (1957) pp. 16-19.
25. *ibid* p. 69.
26. Raphael (1968) p. 186.
27. Althusser (1971) p. 12.

Notes to Chapter Two

1. Fischer (1963) p. 107; Solomon (1973) p. 239.
2. Metchenko (1969) p. 11.
3. The resolution is given in full in Vaughan James (1973) pp. 113-4.

4. Lenin (1967) pp. 21-6.

5. According to Maxim Gorky, Lenin said: "I can't listen to music often, it affects my nerves, it makes me want to say sweet nothings and pat the heads of people who, living in a filthy hell, can create such beauty. But we mustn't pat anyone on the head or we'll get our hand bitten off . . .'. Lenin (1967) p. 226.

6. Erlich (1965) p. 22.

7. Lukacs (1950) p. 121.

8. Quoted in Vaughan James (1973) p. 24.

9. Lenin (1967) p. 28.

10. Slonim (1953) p. 265.

11. Trotsky (1957) p. 219.

12. *ibid.*

13. *ibid.*

14. Metchenko (1969) p. 13.

15. Trotsky (1957) p. 183.

16. Brik (1974) p. 52.

17. Bojko (1972) p. 33.

18. Lissitsky (1967) p. 43.

19. Mayakovsky (1970) pp. 56-7.

20. Vaughan James (1973) pp. 116-9.

21. Brewster (1976) p. 7. See also Brown (1953).

22. Excerpts from Gorky's speech are to be found in Solomon (1973) pp. 243-4 and Gorky (1973).

23. See Brewster (1976) p. 4.

24. Solomon (1973) p. 209.

25. Bakhtin (1968), Volosinov (1973). On Bakhtin, see Kristeva (1972).

26. Solomon (1973) p. 213.

27. Quoted in Biro (1971) p. 27.

28. *ibid* pp. 28-9.

29. Zhdanov (1950) p. 15.

30. On Soviet cinema, see Leyda (1960).

31. Mozhnyagun (1969) p. 246.

32. See "Symposium on the Question of Decadence' in Baxandall 1972) pp. 225-40.

33. For a critical discussion of the problems of the theory from within a ruling Communist Party apparatus, see 'On Socialist Realism' in Baxandall (1972) pp. 240-66.

Notes to Chapter Three

1. Quoted in Gallas (1973), p. 110.

2. Jameson (1971) p. 170.

3. *ibid* p. 172.

4. Lukacs (1971a) p. 7.
5. Lukacs (1950) p. 246.
6. Lukacs (1962) p. 314.
7. See Lukacs (1972b).
8. Benjamin (1973) p. 118.
9. Brecht (1974) p. 48.
10. *ibid* p. 50.
11. Barthes (1964) p. 85.
12. Solomon (1973) pp. 358-9.
13. Gallas (1973) p. 112.
14. Benjamin (1973) p. 91.
15. *ibid* p. 95.
16. For further discussion of these points see Chapter Six, section one.
17. Adorno and Horkheimer (1972).
18. Adorno (1973a) p. 43.
19. Adorno (1973b) p. 81.
20. Adorno (1974) p. 81.
21. Marcuse (1964) p. 65.
22. Marcuse (1969) p. 38.

Notes to Chapter Four

1. Chai Pien (1975) p. 28.
2. Macciocchi (1972) p. 185.
3. Lu Hsun (1973a) p. 163.
4. Quoted in Fei Ling (1973) p. 54.
5. Lu Hsun (1973b) p. 20.
6. Mao Tse Tung (1967) p. 206.
7. Lu Hsun, in Craig (ed., 1975) p. 408.
8. Lu Hsun (1973a) pp. 151, 179.
9. Barthes (1972).
10. Mao Tse Tung (1967) p. 230.
11. Foreign Languages Publishing House, Peking, (1972a) (1972b).
12. Mao Tse Tung (1967) p. 204.
13. *ibid* p. 217.
14. *ibid* p. 216.
15. *ibid* p. 216.
16. *ibid* p. 213.
17. *ibid* p. 208.
18. *ibid* p. 224.
19. Kai-Yu Hsu (1975) p. 94.
20. China Reconstructs, vol 25. no. 8. Quoted in Delmar and Nash (1976/7) p. 74
21. *ibid* p. 73.

Notes to Chapter Five

1. J. Revai, quoted in Lichtheim (1967) p. 78.
2. Sartre (1974) pp. 13-14.
3. In Baxandall (ed.) (1972) p. 226.
4. Sartre (1963) p. 56.
5. Jameson (1971) pp. 217-8.
6. Goldmann (1976) p. 77.
7. Goldmann (1975) p. 7.
8. Goldmann (1976) p. 168.
9. Goldmann (1975) pp. 14-15.
10. Althusser (1969) p. 254.
11. Althusser (1971) p. 219.
12. Althusser (1969) p. 252.
13. 'The Piccolo Teatro: Bertolazzi and Brecht', in Althusser (1969); 'A Letter on Art, in Reply to Andre Daspre' and 'Cremonini, Painter of the Abstract', in Althusser (1971).
14. Althusser (1971) p. 222.
15. Althusser (1969) p. 144.
16. R. Balibar (1974); P. Macherey and E. Balibar (1974).
17. P. Macherey (1977).
18. Macciocchi (1974) p. 224.
19. For contrasting accounts of this controversial concept, see Macciocchi (1974) and Anderson (1977).
20. On this issue, see Hall *et al.*, (1977).
21. Gramsci (1975) p. 122.
22. Anon.: 'The Contented Positivist. M. Foucault and the Death of Man' in the *Times Literary Supplement*, 2.7.70.
23. Barthes (1967) p. 19.
24. Barthes (1964) p. 88.
25. Heath (1972) p. 215.
26. Baudry (1974) p. 23.
27. For an account of television documentary in this perspective see Heath and Skirrow (1977).
28. Kristeva (1976) p. 64.
29. *ibid* p. 68.
30. *ibid* p. 69.
31. *ibid* p. 68.

Notes to Chapter Six

1. Sanchez Vasquez (1973) p. 253.
2. Adorno and Horkheimer (1972) pp. 121-2.
3. *ibid* p. 138.
4. Marcuse (1964) p. 58.

5. *ibid* p. 64.
6. Adorno and Horkheimer (1972) p. 160.
7. Benjamin (1970) p. 223.
8. *ibid* p. 236.
9. *ibid* p. 220.
10. Adorno (1973) p. 66.
11. Enzensberger (1976) p. 27.
12. *ibid* p. 46.
13. *ibid* p. 34.
14. See Eco (1972) and Williams (1974).
15. Balasz (1952).
16. Eikhenbaum (1974) p. 16.
17. See Heath (1973).
18. See Commolli *et al.* (1971), Williams, C. (1972).
19. Cinéthique (1973).
20. *ibid* p. 202.
21. Metz (1975) p. 59.
22. *ibid* p. 14.
23. See Solanas (1972).
24. *ibid* p. 23.
25. Schwarz (1972) p. 220.
26. Adorno (1941).
27. *ibid* p.40.
28. *ibid* p. 42.
29. Sartre (1976) p. 646.

Notes to Chapter Seven

1. Anderson (1965), (1966), Thompson (1965).
2. Thompson (1965) p. 348.
3. See Morton (1952) pp. 149-82.
4. Quoted in Solomon (1973) p. 84.
5. Caudwell (1937) p. 32. '
6. *ibid* pp. 206-7.
7. *ibid* p. 60.
8. Baxandall (ed.) (1972) p. 387.
9. Kettle (1953) vol. 2 p. 61.
10. Berger (1960) p. 208.
11. *ibid* p. 126.
12. Berger (1972) p. 19.
13. *ibid* p. 134.
14. Williams (1977) p. 4.
15. *ibid* p. 13.
16. Coward (1977) p. 78.

BIBLIOGRAPHY

ADORNO, T. W. "On Popular Music', *Studies in Philosophy and Social Sciences.* New York, 1941.

———— with H. Eisler, *Composing for the Films.* New York, 1947.

———— with M. Horkheimer, *Dialectic of Enlightenment.* London, Allen Lane, 1972.

———— *Philosophy of Modern Music.* London, Sheed & Ward, 1973(a)

———— 'Letters to Walter Benjamin', *New Left Review* 81, London, 1973(b)

———— 'On Commitment', *New Left Review* 87/8, London, 1974

ALTHUSSER, L. *For Marx.* London, Allen Lane, 1969.

———— *Lenin and Philosophy and Other Essays.* London, NLB, 1971.

ANDERSON, P. 'Origins of the Present Crisis', *Towards Socialism* (ed. P. Anderson and R. Blackburn). London, Fontana, 1965.

———— 'The Myths of Edward Thompson', *New Left Review* 35, London, 1966

———— 'Components of the National Culture', *Student Power* (ed. R. Blackburn and A. Cockburn). London, Penguin, 1969.

———— 'The Antinomies of Antonio Gramsci', *New Left Review* 100. London, 1976/7.

BAKHTIN, M. *Rabelais and his World.* Cambridge (Mass.), MIT Press, 1968.

BALACZ, B. *The Theory of the Film.* London, Peter Smith, 1952.

BALIBAR, R. *Les Français fictifs: le rapport des styles littéraires au français national.* Paris, Hachette, 1974.

BARKER, F. 'Althusser on Art', *Red Letters* 4. London, 1977.

BARTHES, R. *Essais Critiques.* Paris, Seuil, 1964(a)

———— *On Racine.* New York, Hill & Wang, 1964(b)

———— *Critique et Verité.* Paris, Seuil, 1966.

147

———— *Système de la Mode*. Paris, Seuil, 1967(a)

———— *Writing Degree Zero*. London, Cape Editions, 1967(b).

———— *Elements of Semiology*. London, Cape Editions, 1967(c).

———— 'Rhetoric of the Image', *Working Papers in Cultural Studies* 1. Birmingham, Centre for Contemporary Cultural Studies, 1971.

———— *Mythologies*. London, Fontana, 1972.

———— *S/Z*. London, Cape, 1974.

———— *Image — Music — Text*. London, Fontana, 1977.

BAUDRY, J-L. 'Writing, Fiction, Ideology', *Afterimage* 5. London, 1974.

BAXANDALL, L. *Marxism and Aesthetics: a Selective Annotated Bibliography*. New York, Humanities Press, 1968.

———— editor, *Radical Perspectives in the Arts*. Baltimore and London, Penguin, 1972.

BENJAMIN, W. *Illuminations*. New York, Schocken; London, Cape, 1970.

———— *Understanding Brecht*. London, NLB, 1973.

BERGER, J. *Permanent Red*. London, Methuen, 1960.

———— *Success and Failure of Picasso*. London, Penguin, 1965.

———— with J. Mohr, *A Fortunate Man*. London, Allen Lane, 1967.

———— *The Moment of Cubism*. New York, Pantheon, 1969.

———— *Ways of Seeing*. London, Penguin, 1972.

———— *Selected Essays and Articles*. London, Penguin, 1974.

———— with J. Mohr et al., *A Seventh Man*. London, Penguin, 1975.

BIRO, B. 'Bukharin and Socialist Realism', *Marxist Studies* Vol. 2 No. 1. London, 1970.

BOJKO, S. *New Graphic Design in Revolutionary Russia*. London, Lund Humphries, 1972.

BRECHT, B. ed. J. Willett, *Brecht on Theatre*. London, Methuen, 1964.

———— 'Against Georg Lukacs', *New Left Review* 80. London, 1974.

———— ed. J. Willett and R. Manheim, *Poems*. London, Methuen, 1976.

BREWSTER, B. 'Walter Benjamin', *New Left Review* 48. London 1968.

―――― 'The Soviet State, The Communist Party and the Arts', *Red Letters* 3. London, 1976.

BRIK, O. 'Selected Writings', *Screen* Vol 15. No. 2. London, Society for Education in Film and Television, 1974.

BROWN, E. J. *The Proletarian Episode in Russian Literature 1928-1932*. New York, Octagon, 1970.

BUKHARIN, N. 'Poetry, Politics and Problems of Poetry in the USSR', *Marxism and Art* (ed. M. Solomon). New York, Knopf, 1973. See also Zhdanov et al., *The Soviet Writers' Congress 1934*. London, Lawrence & Wishart, 1977.

CARLES, P. and COMOLLI, J-L. Free Jazz, Black Power. Paris, Champ Libre, 1971.

CAUDWELL, C. *Illusion and Reality*. London, Lawrence & Wishart, 1937. New York, New World, 1963.

――――*Studies in a Dying Culture*. London, Lawrence & Wishart, 1938. New York, Monthly Review Press, 1972.

CAUTE, D. *The Illusion*. London, Andre Deutsch, 1971.

CHAI PIEN *A Glance at China's Culture*. Peking, Foreign Languages Publishing House, 1975.

CHIODI, P. *Sartre and Marxism*. Hassocks, Harvester Press, 1976.

CINÉTHIQUE 'On *Langage et Cinema*', *Screen* Vol 14, No. 1/2. London, Society for Education in Film and Television, 1973.

COMOLLI, J-L. et al. 'Technique et Ideologie', *Cahiers du Cinéma* 229-233. Paris, 1971.

COWARD, R. 'Class, "Culture" and the Social Formation', *Screen* Vol 18, No. 1. London, Society for Education in Film and Television, 1977(a).

―――― & ELLIS, J. *Language and Materialism*. London, Routledge & Kegan Paul, 1977(b).

CRAIG, D. editor, *Marxists on Literature*. London, Penguin, 1975.

DAVIDOV, Y. *The October Revolution and the Arts*. Moscow, Progress Publishers, 1967.

DAY LEWIS, C *A Hope for Poetry*. Oxford, Blackwell, 1936.

DELLA VOLPE, G. *Critica del gusto*. Milan, Feltrinelli, 1960

―――― 'Theoretical Issues of a Marxist Poetics', *Marxism and Art* (ed. B. Lang and F. Williams). New York, McKay, 1972.

DELMAR, R. and NASH, M. 'Breaking With Old Ideas: Recent

Chinese Films', *Screen* Vol. 17 No. 4. London, Society for Education in Film and Television, 1976.

DEMETZ, P. *Marx, Engels and the Poets*. Chicago, 1967.

EAGLETON, T. *Myths of Power: a Marxist Study of the Brontes*. London, Macmillan, 1975.

———— *Literature and Ideology*. London, NLB, 1976(a)

———— Marxism and Literary Criticism. London, Methuen, 1976(b).

ECO, U. *La struttura assente*. Milan, Bompiani 1968.

———— 'Towards a Semiotic Enquiry into the Television Message', *Working Papers in Cultural Studies* 3. Birmingham, Centre for Contemporary Cultural Studies, 1972.

EIKHENBAUM, B. 'Problems of Film Stylistics', *Screen* Vol 15. No. 2. London Society for Education in Film and Television, 1974.

ENZENSBERGER, H. M. *Raids and Reconstructions, Essays on Politics, Crime and Culture*. London, Pluto Press, 1976.

ERLICH, V. *Russian Formalism: History, Doctrine*. The Hague, Mouton, 1965.

FARRELL, J. T. *Selected Essays*. New York, McGraw Hill, 1964.

FEI-LING *Proletarian Culture in China*. London, Association for Radical East Asian Studies, 1973.

FINKLESTEIN, S. *Art and Society*. New York, International, 1947.

———— *Jazz: A People's Music*. New York, International, 1948.

FIORI, G. *Antonio Gramsci: Life of a Revolutionary*. London, NLB, 1970.

FISCHER, E. *The Necessity of Art: A Marxist Approach*. Baltimore and London, Penguin, 1963.

———— *Art Against Ideology*. London, Allen Lane; New York, Braziller, 1969.

FITZPATRICK, S. *The Commissariat of the Enlightenment. Soviet Organisation of Education and the Arts under Lunacharsky, October 1917-1921*. Cambridge, Cambridge University Press, 1970.

FOREIGN LANGUAGES PRESS *Philosophy is no Mystery*. Peking, Foreign Languages Press, 1972(1).

———— *Serving the People with Dialectics*. Peking, Foreign Languages Press, 1972(b)

FOUCAULT, M. *Madness and Civilisation*. London, Tavistock, 1968.

——— *The Order of Things*. London, Tavistock, 1970.

——— 'The Political Function of the Intellectual', *Radical Philosophy* 17. London, 1977.

FRASER, J. *An Introduction to the Thought of Galvano Della Volpe*. London, Lawrence & Wishart, 1976.

GALLAS, H. *Marxistische Literaturtheorie*. Neuwied, Luchterhand, 1971.

——— 'Georg Lukacs and the League of Revolutionary Proletarian Writers', *Working Papers in Cultural Studies* 4. Birmingham, Centre for Contemporary Cultural Studies, 1973.

GARAUDY, R. *D'un realisme sans rivages*. Paris, 1963.

GOLDMANN, L. *The Hidden God*. London, Routledge & Kegan Paul, 1964.

——— 'The Aesthetics of the Young Lukacs', *New Hungarian Quarterly* 45. Budapest, 1972.

——— *Towards a Sociology of the Novel*. London, Tavistock, 1975.

——— *Cultural Creation*. St Louis, Telos Press, 1976.

GORKY, M. 'Speech to the first All-Union Congress of Soviet Writers, 1934', *Marxism and Art* (ed. M. Solomon), New York, Knopf, 1973. See also Zhdanov et al., *The Soviet Writers' Congress, 1934*. London, Lawrence & Wishart, 1977.

GRAMSCI, A. *The Modern Prince and Other Writings*. London, Lawrence & Wishart; New York, International, 1957.

——— *Selections from the Prison Notebooks*. London, Lawrence & Wishart; New York, International, 1971.

HALL, S. & JEFFERSON, R. editors, *Resistance Through Rituals*. London, Hutchinson, 1976.

HALL, S. et al. 'Politics and Ideology: Gramsci', *Working Papers in Cultural Studies* 10. Birmingham, Centre for Contemporary Cultural Studies, 1977.

HEATH, S. *The Nouveau Roman*. London, Elek, 1972.

——— 'Film/Cinetext/Text', Screen Vol. 14 No. 2. London, Society for Education in Film and Television, 1973.

——— and G. Skirrow, 'Television: A World in Action', *Screen* Vol. 18 No. 2. London, Society for Education in Film and Television, 1977.

HESS, H. 'Is There a Theory of Art in Marx?', *Marxism Today* Vol. 17 No. 10. London, 1973.

HOGGART, R. *The Uses of Literacy*. London, Chatto & Windus, 1957.

HORKHEIMER, M. see ADORNO, T. W. (1972)

JAMESON, F. *Marxism and Form*. Princeton, Princeton University Press, 1971

———— *The Prison House of Language*. Princeton, Princeton University Press, 1972.

JAY, M. *The Dialectical Imagination*. Boston, 1973.

JOHNSTON, C. 'Towards a Feminist Film Practice: Some Theses', *Edinburgh Film Festival Magazine*. Edinburgh, 1976.

KAI-YU HSU *The Chinese Literary Scene*. London, Penguin, 1975

KETTLE, A. *An Introduction to the English Novel*. Two volumes. London, Hutchinson, 1953. New York, Harper & Row, 1960.

KRISTEVA, J. 'Ruin of a Poetics', *Twentieth Century Studies* 7/8. Canterbury, 1972.

———— 'Signifying Practice and Mode of Production', *Edinburgh Film Festival Magazine*. Edinburgh, 1976.

———— *On Chinese Women*. London, Marion Boyars, 1977.

LABRIOLA, A. *Essays on the Materialist Conception of History*. Chicago, Kerr, 1908.

LAING, D. *The Sound of our Time*. London, Sheed & Ward, 1969. Chicago, Quadrangle, 1970.

LAING, R. D. and COOPER, D. G. *Reason and Violence*. London, Tavistock, 1964.

LANG, B. and WILLIAMS, F. editors, *Marxism and Art: Writings in Aesthetics and Criticism*. New York, McKay, 1972.

LANE, M. editor, *Structuralism: A Reader*. London, Cape, 1970.

LEIZEROV, N. 'The Scope and Limits of Realism', *Problems of Marxist Aesthetics*. Moscow, Progress Publishers, 1969.

LENIN, V. I. *On Literature and Art*. Moscow, Progress Publishers, 1967.

LEYDA, J. *Kino: A History of the Russian and Soviet Film*. London, 1960.

LICHTHEIM, G. *Lukacs*. London, Fontana, 1970.

LIFSHITZ, M. *The Philosophy of Art of Karl Marx*. London, Pluto, 1973.

LISSITSKY, E. 'The Art of the Book', *New Left Review* 41. London, 1967.

Lu Hsun *Silent China* (ed. G. Yang). Oxford, Oxford University Press, 1973(a).

――― 'Essays', *Chinese Literature* No 5. Peking 1973(b)

Lukacs, G. *Existentialism or Marxism?* London, Hillway, 1948.

――― *Studies in European Realism.* London, Merlin, 1950. New York, Grosset and Dunlap, 1964.

――― *The Historical Novel.* London, Merlin, 1962. Boston, Beacon, 1963.

――― *Writer and Critic.* London, Merlin, 1970. New York, Grosset and Dunlap, 1971.

――― *The Theory of the Novel.* London, Merlin, 1971(a). Cambridge, M.I.T. Press, 1971.

――― *History and Class Consciousness.* London, Merlin, 1971 b).

――― 'Preface to *Art and Society*', *New Hungarian Quarterly* 47, Budapest, 1972(a).

――― 'Labour as a Model of Social Practice', *New Hungarian Quarterly* 47. Budapest, 1972(b).

Macdiarmid, H. *Collected Poems.* New York, Macmillan; Edinburgh, Oliver & Boyd, 1962.

――― *Selected Essays.* London, Cape, 1969. Berkeley, University of California Press, 1970.

――― *Selected Poems.* London, Penguin, 1970.

Macherey, P. *Pour une théorie de la production Littéraire.* Paris, Maspero. 1966.

――― and E. Balibar, 'Sur la littérature comme forme ideologique.' *Littérature* 13. Paris, 1974.

――― 'Interview', *Red Letters* 5. London, 1977.

Macciocchi, M. A. *Daily Life in Revolutionary China.* New York, London, Monthly Review Press, 1972.

――― *Pour Gramsci.* Paris, Seuil, 1974.

Mao-Tse Tung *Selected Readings.* Peking, Foreign Languages Publishing House, 1967.

Marcuse, H. *One Dimensional Man.* Boston, Beacon; London, Sphere, 1964.

――― *Eros and Civilisation.* Boston, Beacon, 1955. London, Sphere, 1969.

――― An Essay on Liberation. Boston, Beacon; London, Allen Lane, 1969.

MAROTHY, J. *Music and the Bourgeois; Music and the Proletarian*. Budapest, 1974.

MARX, K. and ENGELS, F. *The Holy Family*. Moscow, Foreign Languages Press, 1956.

—— *Selected Correspondence*. Moscow, Foreign Languages Press, 1965.

—— *On Literature and Art*. (eds. L. Baxandall and S. Morawski). New York, International General, 1973.

MAYAKOVSKY, V. *How Are Verses Made?* London, Cape Editions, 1970.

McGRATH, J. 'Boom: An Introduction', *New Edinburgh Review* 30. Edinburgh, 1975.

MERTON, R. 'Comment: the Rolling Stones', *New Left Review* 47. London, 1968.

—— with A. Chester, 'For a Rock Aesthetic', *New Left Review* 59. London, 1970.

METCHENKO, A. 'The Basic Principles of Soviet Literature', *Problems of Modern Aesthetics*. Moscow, Progress Publishers, 1969.

METZ, C. 'The Imaginary Signifier', *Screen* Vol. 16 No. 2. London, Society for Education in Film and Television, 1975.

MORRIS, W. *Selected Works* (ed. G. D. H. Cole). London, Nonesuch, 1948. *Selected Writings and Designs* (ed. A. Briggs). London, Penguin, 1962.

MORTON, A. L. *The English Utopia*, London, Lawrence & Wishart, 1952.

MULHERN, F. 'The Marxist Aesthetics of Christopher Caudwell', *New Left Review* 85. London, 1974.

NAIRN, T. 'The Nature of the Labour Party', *Towards Socialism* (eds. R. Blackburn and P. Anderson). London, Fontana, 1965.

NEWTON, F. *The Jazz Scene*. London, Penguin, 1959.

NORTH, J. editor, *New Masses: An Anthology of the Rebel Thirties*. New York, International, 1969.

NOWELL-SMITH, G. 'Gramsci and the "National Popular"', *Screen Education* 22. London, Society for Education in Film and Television, 1977.

OAKLEY, J. 'Althusser and Ideology', *Marxism Today* Vol. 16 No. 8. London, 1971.

PLEKHANOV, G. *Art and Social Life*. Moscow, Progress Publishers, 1957.

PRAWAR, S. S. *Karl Marx and World Literature*. Oxford, Oxford University Press, 1977.

RAPHAEL, M. *The Demands of Art*. Princeton, Princeton University Press; London, Routledge and Kegan Paul, 1968.

REVAI, J. 'A Review of *History and Class Consciousness*', *Theoretical Practice* 1. London, 1971.

ROSENTHAL, M. 'Relative vs. Absolute Criteria in Art', *Artery* 10. London, 1976.

ROWNTREE, J. and ROWNTREE, M. 'The Political Economy of Youth', *International Socialist Journal*. London, 1968.

SANCHEZ VASQUEZ, A. *Art and Society, Essays in Marxist Aesthetics*. New York, Monthly Review Press; London, Merlin, 1973

SARTRE, J-P. *The Problem of Method*. London, Tavistock, 1963.

——— *What is Literature?* New York, Washington Square, 1966.

——— *Between Existentialism and Marxism*. London, NLB, 1974.

——— *The Critique of Dialectical Reason*. London, NLB, 1976.

SHLOVSKY, V. *Mayakovsky and his Circle*. London, Pluto, 1975.

SCHWARS, B. *Music and Musical Life in Soviet Russia*. London, Barrie & Jenkins; New York, Norton, 1972.

SELBOURNE, D. *An Eye to China*. London, Black Liberator Press, 1975.

SEYD, R. 'The Theatre of Red Ladder', *New Edinburgh Review* 30. Edinburgh, 1975.

SLONIM, M. *Modern Russian Literature*. Oxford, Oxford University Press, 1953.

SOLANAS, F. 'For a Third Cinema', *Afterimage* 3. London, 1972.

SOLOMON, M. editor, *Marxism and Art: Essays Classic and Contemporary*. New York, Knopf, 1973.

SOLLERS, P. *Logiques*. Paris, Seuil, 1968.

STALIN, J. *Marxism and Linguistics*. London, Lawrence & Wishart; New York, International, 1951.

STEDMAN JONES, G. 'The Marxism of the Early Lukacs', *New Left Review* 70. London, 1971.

TEL QUEL *Théorie d'ensemble*. Paris, Seuil, 1967.

THERBORN, G. 'Frankfurt Marxism', *New Left Review* 63. London, 1970.

THOMPSON, E. P. 'The Long Revolution', *New Left Review* 9-10. London, 1961.

———— 'The Peculiarities of the English', *Socialist Register*. London, Merlin, 1965.

———— *William Morris, Romantic to Revolutionary*. London, Merlin, 1977.

THOMSON, G. *Marxism and Poetry*. London, Lawrence & Wishart, 1946.

TIMPANERO, S. 'Considerations on Materialism', *New Left Review* 85. London, 1974.

TODOROV, T. editor, *Theorie de la littérature: textes des formalistes russes*. Paris, Seuil, 1965.

TROTSKY, L. *Literature and Revolution*. New York, Russell and Russell, 1957.

VAUGHAN JAMES, C. *Soviet Socialist Realism. Theory and Doctrine*. London, Macmillan, 1973.

VOLOSINOV, V. N. *Marxism and the Philosophy of Language*. New York, London, Seminar Press, 1973.

WEISS, P. *Notes on the Cultural Life of the Democratic Republic of Vietnam*. London, Calder, 1971.

WELLEK, R. and WARREN, A. *Theory of Literature*. New York, Harcourt, Brace and World, 1949.

WILLENER, A *The Action-Image of Society*. London, Tavistock, 1970.

WILLIAMS, C. 'The Deep Focus Question', *Screen* Vol. 13 no. 1. London, Society for Education in Film and Television, 1972.

WILLIAMS, R. *Culture and Society*. London, Chatto and Windus, 1958.

———— *The Long Revolution*. London, Chatto & Windus, 1961.

———— *Orwell*. London, Fontana, 1971.

———— 'Base and Superstructure', *New Left Review* 82. London, 1973.

———— *Television: Technology and Cultural Form*. London, Fontana, 1974.

———— *Marxism and Literature*. Oxford, Oxford University Press, 1977.

WITT, H. editor, *Brecht as they knew him*. London, Lawrence and Wishart, 1975.

WOLLEN, P. *Signs and Meaning in the Cinema*. London, Secker and Warburg, 1969.

——— 'Counter Cinema: *Vent D'Est*', *Afterimage* 4. London, 1972.

ZHDANOV, A. A. *On Literature, Music and Philosophy*. London, Lawrence & Wishart; New York, International, 1950.

——— with M. Gorky et al. *The Soviet Writers' Congress 1934*. London, Lawrence & Wishart, 1977.

ZITTA, V. *Lukacs' Marxism*. The Hague, Mouton, 1964.

INDEX